STORY:
The Heart of the Matter

edited by
Dr Maggie Butt

Greenwich Exchange, London

STORY: The Heart of the Matter
edited by Dr Maggie Butt
© 2007 Copyright in each contribution is held by the individual author.

First published in Great Britain in 2007
All rights reserved

Printed and bound by Q3 Digital/Litho, Loughborough
Tel: 01509 213456
Typesetting and layout by Albion Associates, London
Tel: 020 8852 4646
Cover design by December Publications, Belfast
Tel: 028 90286559

Cover: © Alamy Images

Greenwich Exchange Website: www.greenex.co.uk

Cataloguing in Publication Data is available from the British Library

ISBN-13: 978-1-871551-93-8
ISBN-10: 1-871551-93-5

*Grateful thanks to all the contributors,
to my colleagues and students at Middlesex University
and to Helena Blakemore.
And, as always, to my family.*

Contents

Contributors

Sarah Boston is a documentary director who has made films for the BBC, Channel 4, ITV and Sky. Her documentaries have covered a wide range of subjects including a study of racism in football (*Great Britain United*, C4); the work of BBC foreign correspondent John Simpson (*Behind The Reporting Line*, BBC); the life and work of Joris Ivens (*Too Much Reality*, BBC) and a film (*The Grapes of Wrath Revisited*, C4) which retraced the journey of Steinbeck's novel 50 years after its publication. Most recently she directed a feature-length, independent documentary, *Cruel Separation*, about the lives of four women whose husbands all died in Pinochet's military coup. In 2006 this film won Best International Documentary at the Viña de Mai festival. Sarah is also an author and her works include *Women Workers and The Trades Unions* and the award-winning *Will, My Son*. She is currently a senior lecturer at Middlesex University teaching documentary production.

Dr Maggie Butt is the Chair of the National Association of Writers in Education, and head of Media at Middlesex University, where she has taught Creative Writing since 1990 and is a University Teaching Fellow. Following an English degree, she trained as a newspaper reporter, worked as a journalist in Devon and in London, then entered BBC Television where she researched, wrote, directed and produced features and documentaries, including films for BBC 2's *Forty Minutes* and *Timewatch* series. Her creative writing PhD focused on English fiction, and she has also written for children. She is involved in the promotion of creative writing at a national and international level through the National Association of Writers in Education. Her poems are widely published in magazines and on the internet. Her poetry pamphlet, *Quintana Roo*, was published by Acumen in 2003 and her full collection, *Lipstick*, was published by Greenwich Exchange in 2007.

James Martin Charlton was born in Romford, Essex in 1966 and educated in the comprehensive school system. His play *Fat Souls* won the 1992 International Playwriting Festival at Warehouse Theatre, Croydon, where it premiered in 1993. His subsequent plays include: *The World & His Wife* (White Bear, 1995); *Groping in the Dark* (Mermaid, 1996); *Coming Up* (Warehouse, 1997); and *Divine Vision*, about William Blake (Swedenborg Hall, 2000). In 2001, his play *ecstasy + GRACE* hit national newspaper headlines due to its graphic, uncompromising portrait of paedophilia and moral degeneracy. Recent work includes the country house comedy *I Really Must be Getting Off* (White Bear, 2005) and a new play based on an episode in the life of Noel Coward, to be premiered in London in the near future. He wrote and directed the short film, *Apeth*, completed in 2006, as well as writing two more short films, *Best Shot* (2006) and *Emotional Tribunal* (2007). Two feature scripts, *Take Me In* and *London* are currently in development. He lectures in Scriptwriting on the Creative Writing programme at Middlesex University.

Sally Pomme Clayton is a storyteller and writer and has been performing for adults and children since 1984. She founded *The Company of Storytellers* with Ben Haggarty and Hugh Lupton in 1985, and together they have spearheaded the revival of storytelling in the UK, creating unique and groundbreaking performances. Sally Pomme Clayton performs throughout Britain and internationally and has toured with The British Council in Europe and Central Asia. In 2003 she created *The Tales of the Seven Princesses* for Chichester Festival Theatre. In 2004 she was commissioned by BBC Radio 3 and Apples and Snakes to create a spoken word piece for WOMAD. In 2004 she wrote and performed *Rama and Sita – Path of Flames* for The Unicorn Children's Theatre. During 2005-2006 she was consultant for the British Library *Inside Story* project.She has published collections of stories and written plays for radio and theatre. Her latest book is *Tales Told in Tents – Stories from Central Asia*, published by Frances Lincoln. She is currently writing a book based on her version of Ramayana. She lectures on world oral traditions and creative writing at Middlesex University.

Professor Philip Gross is a writer of many parts – from Faber and Bloodaxe poet to writer of fiction for young people. He has published science fiction, haiku and schools opera libretti, plays and radio short stories. His adult poetry, up to and including the Whitbread shortlisted, *The Wasting Game*, is collected in *Changes of Address* (2001) and since then Bloodaxe has also published *Mappa Mundi* (2003) and *The Egg of Zero* (2006). Recent novels, from Oxford University Press, include *Going For Stone* (2002), *The Lastling* (2003) and *The Storm Garden* (2006). He has been a writer in schools for 20 years. In 2004 he became Professor of Creative Writing at Glamorgan University where his research interest is collaboration – a central strand of his writing life – where he has worked with other writers (*The Air Mines Of Mistila* (1988) with Sylvia Kantaris) and with composers, dancers and visual artists. *The Abstract Garden* (Old Stile Press, 2006) is a book-length project with engraver Peter Reddick.

Dr Mary Hammond began her career as a writer/researcher for the mass-market publisher Book Creations Inc., New York, and is currently Senior Lecturer in English at the University of Southampton, where she is responsible for the development of Creative Writing programmes. She is the author of *Reading, Publishing and the Formation of Literary Taste in England, 1880-1914* (Ashgate, 2006); co-author of *Creative Writing: A Workbook with Readings*, ed. Linda Anderson (Routledge, 2005); co-editor of *Publishing in the First World War* (Palgrave, 2007) and *Books Without Borders*, Vols. 1 & 2 (Palgrave, 2008) and has written numerous articles on the literature and publishing and reading practices of the 19th and early 20th centuries, including a chapter in the new *Cambridge Companion to Literature 1830-1914*. She has written and taught Creative Writing courses for the Open College Network, the University of Southampton, Middlesex University and the Open University.

Professor Graeme Harper (who writes, creatively, as Brooke Biaz) is Professor of Creative Writing and Director of the National Institute for Excellence in the Creative Industries at the University of Wales, Bangor. His latest books are *Small Maps of the World* (Parlor, 2006),

Teaching Creative Writing (Continuum, 2006), *Moon Dance* (Parlor, 2007), and *Creative Writing Studies: Practice, Theory, Pedagogy* (MLM, 2007), ed. with Jeri Kroll. He is Editor-in-Chief of *New Writing: The International Journal for the Practice and Theory of Creative Writing* (MLM). He holds doctorates from the University of Technology, Sydney and the University of East Anglia. His new critical monograph, *What is Creative Writing?* is to be published by MLM in 2008.

Russell Kane (born Russell Grineau) is a writer, stand-up comic, actor, TV interviewer and presenter. He has done many things en route: door-to-door vacuum cleaner salesman; door-to-door frozen food salesman; library assistant; Rolex watch dealer; graduate of Middlesex University with a first in Literature and Writing; completing half an MA in Modernism at the University of London; Junior/Middleweight/Senior then Head Copywriter in an Ad Agency; then, finally, The Funny Business – all of this while the little workaholic was in his twenties. In 2003 he finally mustered the courage to eat a box of Imodium, get on stage and perform his first stand-up gig. Within four months he was signed by Avalon, who manage Frank Skinner, Harry Hill et al. Since then he has won the Laughing Horse New Act of The Year in 2004, and in 2006 was nominated for a Perrier Award for his debut solo Edinburgh Show 'The Theory of Pretension'.

Current projects are: working as the face of a 2006-launched digital channel FIVE US – including co-writing all the material related to his appearances; working on a new Shakespearean language idea wherein Essex Characters speak in blank verse; and also working with 2006-launched Channel Four Radio on satirical sketches. Other than that, he's just chilling really.

Dr Neil McCaw teaches English and Creative Writing at the University of Winchester, where he is also the Director of the BA in Creative Writing and MA in Creative and Critical Writing. He has written and lectured on various aspects of Victorian culture, crime fiction, creative writing pedagogy, and is Academic Director of the Arthur Conan Doyle Collection – the most wide-ranging Conan Doyle and Sherlock Holmes collection in the world. His publications include

George Eliot and Victorian Historiography (Macmillan, 2000), *Writing Irishness in Nineteenth-Century British Culture* (Ashgate, 2004), and *How to Read Texts* (Continuum, 2007); he is presently working on a series of Sherlock Holmes adaptations for children.

Dr Farah Mendlesohn is the UK's first Reader in Fantasy and Science Fiction, and President of the International Association of the Fantastic in the Arts. She has been editor of *Foundation: The International Review of Science Fiction* for six years (2001-2007), and was Chair of the Science Fiction Foundation from 1998-2004. In 2005 she and her co-editor Edward James won the Hugo Award for the *Cambridge Companion to Science Fiction*. She has recently published a book on the British fantasy writer, Diana Wynne Jones, and her book *Rhetorics of Fantasy* will be out in 2007. Her latest project is a wide-ranging study of science fiction for children.

Professor Andrew Melrose is Professor of Children's Writing and Director of the MAs in Writing for Children and Creative and Critical Writing at the University of Winchester. He has over a hundred writing credits for films, books, songs, chapters and articles, including *The Story Keepers* animation series for ITV and international broadcast, *Write for Children* (Routledge Falmer, 2002); *Storykeeping* (Paternoster, 2002) and *Magic Mr Edison* (Random House, 2004). He is presently developing a book, an exhibition and a film entitled *Kyoto* – a big story about a boy and a little bear – and a little story about global warming; writing a pre-teen novel on Iraq, and *Palace Pier Blues* is his first novel for grown-ups, due out at the same time as this collection.

Helena Nelson is a poet, essayist, critic and further education lecturer. Her first book-length poetry collection, *Starlight on Water*, was joint prize-winner of the Jerwood First Collection Prize in 2003. A trustee of St Anza, Scotland's poetry festival, she reviews for various magazines, including *The Dark Horse*, *PN Review*, *Poetry Review*, *Magma* and *Ambit*. She has also contributed monographs on W.H. Davies, Robert Nye, Norman Cameron and Ruth Pitter to Scribner's *British Writers* series. In 2005 she launched *HappenStance*, a small press imprint, specialising in poetry chapbooks. *HappenStance* also publishes *Sphinx*, a magazine which runs features and interviews with poetry publishers and poets, and which maintains a special interest in chapbook publications.

Dr Sarah Niblock is what might loosely be described as a 'hackademic', one of a new breed of journalism practitioner-academics. She has worked in journalism for nearly 20 years as a regional and national news reporter, and she wrote features for *Cosmopolitan* and *Company* for four years. Sarah is the author of several books including *Inside Journalism* (1996), *News Production: Theory and Practice* (2006, co-authored with David Machin). She has published chapters in *Print Journalism: A Critical Introduction* (2005), *Reading Sex and the City* (2004) and *Feminist Visual Culture* (2000). A further book, on journalism ethics as portrayed in cinema since the dawn of film, is in production. Sarah has an MA in Visual Culture and holds, it is believed, the world's first PhD on the rock star Prince and his appeal to female fans in the mid-1980s.

Dr David Rain was born in Australia and has lived in Ireland and England since 1990. Writing under the pseudonym Tom Arden, he began his publishing career with *The Orokon*, a million-word, five-volume sequence of novels comprising *The Harlequin's Dance* (1997), *The King and Queen of Swords* (1998), *Sultan of the Moon and Stars* (1999), *Sisterhood of the Blue Storm* (2000) and *Empress of the Endless Dream* (2001). Set in an imaginary 18th-century world, this darkly comic fantasy epic has been variously described as "grotesque", "marvellously camp", "a sprawling baroque tapestry", and "a feverish cross between Georgette Heyer and Mervyn Peake". Other publications as Tom Arden include the *Doctor Who* book *Nightdreamers* (2002) and the offbeat gothic novels *Shadow Black* (2002) and *The Translation of Bastian Test* (2005). David has also written short stories, columns, reviews, and academic criticism. He studied English Literature at the University of Adelaide and completed a PhD thesis on the 18th-century novel, *Clarissa*, by Samuel Richardson. For seven years he lectured in English at Queen's University of Belfast. He was the inaugural Royal Literary Fund Fellow at the University of Brighton, and is presently Programme Leader in Creative and Media Writing at Middlesex University.

Michelene Wandor is a playwright, poet, fiction writer and musician. She is the first woman playwright to have had a drama on one of the National Theatre's main stages – *The Wandering Jew*, in 1987, the same year her adaptation of *The Belle of Amherst* won an International Emmy for Thames TV. Her prolific radio drama includes original radio plays and dramatisations (novels by Dostoevsky, Jane Austen, George Eliot, Rudyard Kipling, Sara Paretsky and Margaret Drabble), many nominated for awards. Her books on contemporary theatre include *Postwar British Drama: Looking Back in Gender*. In 2002 she received a Millennium Lottery Fund Award, to make a CD of the music of Salamone Rossi, an early 17th-century Jewish Mantuan composer. Her poetry, *Gardens of Eden Revisited*, and her short stories, *False Relations*, are published by Five Leaves. She is completing a book about Creative Writing and holds a Royal Literary Fund Fellowship since 2004. Her new poetry collection, *Musica Transalpina*, was a Poetry Book Society Recommendation for Spring, 2006 and *The Music of the Prophets*, a long narrative poem about the resettlement of the Jews in England in 1655-6, was published in 2007. Her most recent dramatisation for radio is *Lady Chatterley's Lover*, a two-part Classic Serial for Radio 4, broadcast in September, 2006. Her book, *The Author is not Dead, Merely Somewhere Else: Creative Writing Reconceived* is to be published by Methuen in 2008.

Introduction

Magic and Imagination

Maggie Butt

How many stories do you think you've heard this week? In novels, films, magazine articles, news stories, documentaries, jokes, excuses, cartoons, songs, soaps, interviews, eavesdropping, essays, dreams, paintings, lies, poetry, rumours, plays, dreams or good old gossip? And why do you think we never get bored of stories, but are always hungry for more?

An insatiable appetite for stories is hard-wired into human beings, without any appreciable evolutionary benefit (rather like pleasure in music, or enjoyment of dancing). Telling stories and arranging life into stories is a universal and timeless need of the human psyche. There isn't any historical time or any place on earth where people have not told stories. Real life is muddled, largely without clearly delineated beginnings and endings (apart from the ultimate ones), so we need stories to impose order on the chaos, to explain our lives to ourselves. Auden wrote, "Every normal human being is interested in two kinds of worlds: the Primary, everyday world which he knows through his senses and a Secondary world or worlds which he not only can create in his imagination, but also cannot stop creating." [1]

Almost as strange as the unquenchable thirst we have to consume stories, is the desire some of us have to tell them, as author, scriptwriter, poet, journalist, oral storyteller or comedian. Sometimes this urge is born in us, sometimes it is acquired later. At times of great stress many people use poetry to help explore (or explain to themselves) the story of their own lives – to break the chaotic nature of existence into small, manageable narrative chunks.

Throughout my life, I have written in a variety of forms and genres, and have never been able to stop. I began writing stories and poems at the age of seven, pretty much as soon as I knew how to read and hold a pencil. (I also chugged my way relentlessly through the public library.) In my teens I told stories to the children I babysat for. I deconstructed other people's stories through my English degree, joined a newspaper and dashed off dozens of stories a day, moved to the BBC and slowed the pace with filmed documentaries, had children and wrote children's tales, began teaching and explored fiction for my PhD, and most recently returned to my first love of poetry. But I'm not content to play with words in the privacy of my own home. I have the urge to share what I write – in newspapers, on TV, in books and poetry magazines, and that wonderful web of stories around the globe – the internet.

I don't know why I write, but I do know that stories are important, and have been, back as far as we can go. Australian Aborigines have a tradition of stories being handed to a new keeper in every generation. These stories, carefully guarded and handed down over thousands of years, are more than free entertainment. They help to explain the chaos of living to those who hear them, and sometimes have real practical benefits, for example by guiding each new generation to the places where water can be found in a desert. In Italo Calvino's book *Invisible Cities*, [2] the Great Khan wants to know about reality. Marco Polo suggests that stories offer an understanding of the darkness.

Many of the stories we know and love in the West are very old, and very well travelled, carried by merchants and adventurers who criss-crossed the globe long before air travel. A Chinese story, written down in the 9th century, features a heroine with very small feet, dressed in kingfisher feathers which were conjured by magic. She goes to a feast, where she loses her slipper ... Our modern *Cinderella* story makes more sense when you know it may originate from a culture where the smallness of women's feet was the principal sign of beauty. But it resonates for all times and places as the story of rags to riches. The Ancient Greek story *Cupid & Psyche* changes as it travels through time, until it becomes a story whose theme is the possibility that someone will see though your disfigurement and love you – the story we know as *Beauty and the Beast* and which is meaningful to every new generation.

Stories are the strongest bonds we have in common across nation, race and language. The stories themselves may change as they migrate, taking on new clothes to fit the culture or the age, but they remind us of the unchanging qualities of human nature, which we all share. Here's the start of a story: a super-human king misuses his power and oppresses his people (including claiming first right of sexual intercourse with every bride), but an 'uncivilised' man from the country comes to the city to sort him out ... This could be a modern story, but it's the *Epic of Gilgamesh*, a story written down on 12 clay tablets in Cuneiform script about 5000 years ago in Sumeria (modern Iraq). This epic adventure is the world's oldest written story, by the world's oldest known author – Sin-liqe-unninni. Here's another tale: a long-haired, charismatic man leads all the women from a city up a hillside to have a wild drunken party, while the city officials remain powerless ... This is the story of *The Bacchae*, told to us by Euripides. The long-haired man is Dionysus, the god of wine and religious ecstasy, part of the Olympic Pantheon of the Ancient Greeks. But it could be a cult anywhere, anytime.

Folk tales have stood the test of time because they have a universal message. Early versions of *Little Red Riding Hood* don't have a friendly woodcutter to set everything right. Little Red Riding Hood gets eaten by the wolf. End of story. And a simple message – 'the woods are dangerous places'. And today this story still has powerful metaphorical significance, although the dangerous woods might have become traffic or city centres, and the wolf may have become 'stranger danger'.

Folk tales acknowledge the universal difficulty and unfairness of life for some people. They often begin with broken families, with deaths of parents, with a world in turmoil. They understand the power of language, that a threatening phone call can make you tremble and that the old saying, 'Sticks and stones can break my bones but names can never hurt me', simply isn't true. So folk tales are full of curses, spells and incantations – the power of the word. These stories help us understand that others have suffered as we suffer, and – thanks to the storyteller's art – often win through to better times. As Robert McKee says, "Stories are equipment for living".[3]

Stories have long been used to bring abstract ideas to life. The major world holy books are filled with stories, which often make a moral point. The message of Noah and the Flood – if you live a God-fearing life you can be saved from catastrophe; the message of David and Goliath – the weak can defeat the strong with the help of God. But how much more memorable the morals become when dressed in these great stories. The teaching of Jesus was usually done in parables, stories which have become part of Western culture, like the Good Samaritan, which urges us to help strangers in trouble, even if they are our enemies. Stories like these can and do change lives, and can even change the world – for better or worse. If the assemblers of the Biblical Genesis story had only included the version in Chapter One which contains the translated words, "So God created man in his own image, in the image of God created he him; male and female created he them", and not added another version in Chapter Two which retells the story with different details, saying that God took one of Adam's ribs and created woman from that, we might have been spared a few thousand years of misogyny.

Stories are powerful because they represent the imagination in action. Imagination comes from the same root word as magic. The power of the imagination – like magic – can bring about change. Stories can change the way people feel and act. And I'm not just thinking of the stories which form the basis of the major world religions. I'm thinking of Dickens, bringing a range of social ills to the attention of the public; of the poetry of Wilfred Owen and the other First World War poets who changed forever our idea that war is clean and heroic; of the novel *All Quiet on the Western Front* [4] which helped a generation see that Germans are not so different after all; of the 1960s drama documentary *Cathy Come Home* [5] which exposed problems of homelessness and led to the setting up of Shelter; of Michael Buerk's BBC report from Ethiopia in October 1984 which showed the world the full horror of the famine in Ethiopia and inspired Band Aid, Live Aid and later Comic Relief; of the bestselling novel *To Kill a Mockingbird* [6] and the movie *Guess Who's Coming to Dinner* [7] which did more to make people examine their own racism than any number of laws and demonstrations; of Michael Moore's groundbreaking documentaries. The list could go on and on.

So how can we turn our urge to make stories into an ability to make stories which change lives? (Our own or other people's.) Or if we aren't so ambitious, how can we at least draw people into the world of our stories and connect with the imagination of the recipient? The essence of storymaking is the conjuring up of a world so vividly that it seems to live in the mind of the listener or reader.

Many books have been written about the essential components of a good story, but the simplest definition might be that something ought to happen. To make it into a newspaper, that 'something' which 'happens' has to be quite unusual. In the crime-free Devon town where I did my journalist training, we once had a front page headline which ran "Milk Bottles Stolen from Doorstep". It was a crime-wave unusual enough to make the front page. Yet in America now even school shootings have become so commonplace that they don't make it onto national news. The old adage is true: 'Dog bites man' isn't news, but 'man bites dog' is. But even though it might not be newsworthy, 'dog bites man' may still be the kernel of a story, with a little dash of imagination, and a mind that asks the question 'what if?' What if the dog is an old man's only companion and he can't face having the dog put down, so runs away with him? ... what if the dog is the last remaining example of its breed? ... what if the man is a child on holiday who dies of rabies? ... Something has happened and it has moved from cause to effect. E.M. Forster wrote, "We have defined a story as a narrative of events arranged in their time-sequence. A plot is also a narrative of events, the emphasis falling on causality. 'The king died and then the queen died' is a story. 'The king died, and then the queen died of grief' [8] is a plot."

Film producers often ask for a one-line summary of a plot. It is said that if you can't sum up your movie in one sentence you haven't found the heart of it. This summary gives the gist of what happens, what makes it a real story rather than a chain of events. My first news editor advised me that the core of a story (all encapsulated in a pithy 25 word 'intro') is the bit which pops into your mind when you sit down in the pub to tell your friends, "Hey, guess what happened ..." That 'What happened' might be ' ... a young alien got left behind on earth and a child found him and helped him call home' or 'three brothers were killed in action so the army decided to find the fourth brother, and bring him home to his mother ...' or 'an unsuitable nun helped a singing family escape from the Nazis'.

The kernel of the idea, with an unusual 'something' which 'happens' and a sequence of cause and effect, is step one. It presupposes characters and a setting and possibly even a structure. But it doesn't matter how wonderful the idea is if you can't bring it alive for its audience. One of the most exciting things about storymaking is the connection between the teller and the hearer – whether those are friends in a pub, an audience in a comedy club or movie-goers. That connection is harder to see in the private reading of a novel or a poem, (and many poems are meditations rather than stories) but a poem can illustrate, in a small space, that relationship between writer and reader. A poem may capture the central moment, the climax of a story, almost freeze-framing it (a photograph rather than a movie) leaving the reader to fill in the narrative which streams out in both directions, before and after this moment. For instance, in my haiku 'November':

> A flurry of leaves
> A darkness of mornings
> A slip of pavements

The reader is left to imagine the old lady with the shopping bags who falls on the wet leaves – or whatever else it was that you may have conjured. All you were given was one verb, "slip" as a clue to the story. You did the rest.

In my 'Halloween' poem, I lightly sketch the setting, the characters, and hint at the possible 'somethings' which might happen:

> The Underground girls are bold with lager,
> dressed to kill: fishnets, black lips, piercings,
> spiders' webs etched on whitened skin;
> they ride the rails to trick or treat.

The reader's imagination supplies the sounds, the smells, the possible naughty or salacious endings to the evening. These poems are obviously not world-changing stories, but simple examples to show how poetry can be a highly interactive form of storytelling, in which the reader's imagination is as crucial as the words on the page.

Because that's the crux of storytelling: the connection between the person who makes the story and the one who reads or hears or sees it: the laughter in a comedy club; the sense of being carried away when you lose yourself in a novel or film; the anger, or outrage, or sorrow, or joy which a well-told news story or documentary can unleash. Stories bond us together; they are one of the best ways we have to share experience. They help us explain the world to ourselves, make order out of chaos, while reinforcing the connections between us. Stories take us out of our own narrow lives and launch us into the lives of others.

In this book, writers share their personal ideas about storymaking, gained from experience as writers, readers and creative-writing tutors in British universities. This book doesn't tell you how to write a play, or novel or poem, as if it were a cookbook and there were a certain recipe for success, but offers you insights which are the fruit of years of experience. The centrality of story runs across forms and genres, so what's said here about joke telling could be applied to novel writing, what's written about immersion reporting might be applied to playwriting, what's said about storytelling has been applied to essay writing. They examine some of the ways we can make that all-important connection between the writer and the audience – how to make the magic happen.

Dive in, and make your own story.

Notes
[1] W.H. Auden, *Afterword* – from *The Visionary Novels of George MacDonald*, ed. Anne Freemantle, (Farrar, Straus & Giroux Inc.,1954).
[2] Italo Calvino, *Le Citta Invisibli* (Giulio Einaudi Editore, 1972). English version translated William Weaver, 1974.
[3] Robert McKee, *Story: Substance, Structure, Style and the Principles of Screenwriting* (Regan Books, 1997).
[4] Erich Maria Remarque, *Im Westen Nichts Neues*, 1929.
[5] *Cathy Come Home* was screened on BBC1 on 16th December 1966. It was written by Jeremy Sandford, produced by Tony Garnett and directed by Ken Loach.
[6] Harper Lee, *To Kill a Mockingbird* (Harper Collins, 1960) won Pulitzer prize for fiction, 1961.
[7] *Guess Who's Coming to Dinner* (Columbia Pictures, 1967). Written by William Rose, directed by Stanley Kramer, starring Spencer Tracy, Katharine Hepburn, Sydney Poitier and Katharine Houghton. (Inter-racial marriage was still illegal in 17 southern US states in 1967.)
[8] E.M. Forster, *Aspects of the Novel*, 1927. A published collection of the Clark lectures delivered at Trinity College, Cambridge in 1927.

1

Believing Stories

David Rain

We believe stories. Or want to.
Suspension of disbelief – an audience's willing surrender to the illusions of fiction – is a key concept in storytelling. How does a story grip us, hold us? When a story takes us over, we're *lost in a book*. It's as if we're *there*. Of course we know we're just lying in bed, or sitting on the train. We aren't really in Middle Earth or Middlemarch or 'Salem's Lot. But the better the book – or the better it is for us – the more the real world retreats, the more we care about what is, after all, a species of dream. What can this tell us about how to write?

It's often said that you can't write fiction well unless you read a lot of it, too. This is true – because you need, even if only instinctively, to understand what reading does to a reader. Somerset Maugham said once that to indulge in fantasy was to acknowledge defeat in the face of reality. [1] He was right, I suppose. But all fiction is fantasy, a mechanism of imagined belief. That's what it's *for.*

Reading fiction, when it goes well, is an experience of *immersion* in an imaginative world. Think of any notable novelist or short-story writer – Austen, Balzac, Poe, Dickens, Conrad, Woolf, Graham Greene, Anne Rice, Anne Tyler, add your own – and what you think of is seldom this or that storyline so much as the characteristic milieu or world evoked in that writer's work.

The claim that some writers – the good ones – are concerned

fundamentally with the real world, with commenting on society, while others reprehensibly manufacture an escapist dream-world, stands up to little scrutiny. Whether it looks like life or not, Storyworld is always a dream. The desire for story is the desire for a substitute world. That this may illuminate the real world is undeniable, but this is seldom the reason for its appeal. *Macbeth* is a good story because it is atmospheric, dramatic and frightening, not because it teaches us Scottish history, or tells us that too much ambition may not be a good idea.

Samuel Richardson's *Pamela: Or, Virtue Rewarded* (1740) is the first example in English literature of the 'bestselling novel'. Learn about *Pamela*, and you learn about every bestseller since. You also learn how to write a novel.

Pamela is the story of a servant-girl who resists repeated seduction attempts by the handsome young son of her mistress, bringing him in time to propose marriage. Whether Pamela was really the humble, virtuous maiden she appeared to be, or a designing minx with her eye on the main chance, has long been a source of debate. What was never in doubt was the novel's success. It was immediate and overwhelming. Not only was *Pamela* twice dramatized, it was also made into an opera; there were commentaries, parodies, unauthorised sequels; scenes from the novel were illustrated in a series of paintings by the artist Joseph Highmore, and engravings sold in sets; at the pleasure gardens at Vauxhall, pavilions were decorated with *Pamela* displays; characters from *Pamela* were reproduced in waxwork; there were *Pamela* teacups, even fans ornamented with a *Pamela* motif.

Why was *Pamela* so successful?
Pamela is a novel in letters, or 'epistolary novel' – Pamela, supposedly, is writing home to her parents, describing her experiences in the home of her rich employer. Of course, epistolary form is in part simply an 'authenticating' device – one of those tricks typically used by early novelists to encourage suspension of disbelief. Defoe's *Robinson Crusoe* (1719) posed as the real-life autobiography of a shipwrecked sailor. Similarly, Richardson presented himself as the 'editor' of a real collection of letters. But the significance of the form goes deeper. Of particular importance is that each letter is

supposed to have been written at a different time. When writing any given letter, the writer cannot know what his or her future holds. Richardson's term for this technique was *writing to the moment*.[2]

If we ask how *Pamela* differed from earlier epistolary novels, one simple but revealing answer is that it is much longer. Early novels were typically short – or, if they ran into hundreds of pages, crowded into those pages were a large number of sketchily-described adventures.[3] Defoe's *Moll Flanders* (1722) is typical; *Robinson Crusoe*, which depicts Crusoe's survival on his island in extraordinary detail, is a rare exception. Richardson loves detail. The fact that Pamela narrates her story through letters means that each situation in which she finds herself – she is nearly raped time and again, variously persecuted, pursued, imprisoned – is immediate to her, vividly and powerfully emotive, at the time of writing.

Few writers nowadays tackle the novel-in-letters. But Richardson's concept of *writing to the moment* remains crucial. "Dramatise, dramatise!" said Henry James,[4] and he meant the same thing. Pamela doesn't just *tell*. She *shows*.

Pamela is a novel filled with *incidents*. Literary fiction at its highest or most abstracted typically makes incident less significant than mood or atmosphere: Proust, Joyce, Woolf. But it's still about being there – perhaps, supremely so. One of my favourite books is *The Magic Mountain* (1924) by Thomas Mann. It's a masterpiece of procrastination. Almost nothing happens, and yet the book, about a young man's protracted stay in a Swiss sanatorium, has hallucinatory power. This is because everything in Mann is *seen*, everything *felt*. The author projects himself so fully into each situation, renders it so scrupulously, that it becomes part of one's own experience.

This suggests something about how to invent stories – how to *dream them up*.

How much planning should a dreamer do?

You can't go far in creative writing land nowadays without hearing about Joseph Campbell and the hero's journey. Campbell (1904-87) was an American folklorist who studied traditional stories from around the world in order to find a "monomyth", or master-narrative, underlying them all. The hero's journey, as presented by Campbell, is a story of maturation: the hero, first seen living an unsatisfactory, "ordinary" life, receives a "call to adventure" or challenge, and has to go on a real or implicit quest; the story leads to the final overcoming of an obstacle which not only brings rewards to the hero but benefits the wider world. Laid out in his book *The Hero With a Thousand Faces* (1949), Campbell's principles of story-structure were followed by filmmaker George Lucas in the original *Star Wars* (1977);[5] later, the uses of the hero's journey for screenwriting were codified in a widely-used handbook, a sort of Hollywood Bible, Christopher Vogler's *The Writer's Journey* (1992).

The belief that structure offers a magic key to storytelling has only grown in popularity since then. Vogler's handbook was followed by Robert McKee's *Story* (1997), with its elaborate graphs and tables; while Christopher Booker's *The Seven Basic Plots* (2004) revives at exhaustive length the sort of story-taxonomy which dates back at least to Georges Polti's *The Thirty-Six Dramatic Situations* (1921). For the ultimate plot-by-numbers experience, try *Plots Unlimited* (1995) by Tom Sawyer and Arthur David Weingarten; also released as a computer programme, this is a sort of telephone directory of scenarios and character-types with numbered keys to help us combine elements into myriad different plots. *Plots Unlimited* is a brilliant organisational exercise, admirable as a testament to the authors' industriousness – and wholly useless to any writer beyond the most desperate hack.

It's true that many stories, particularly in popular fiction, conform to models such as the hero's journey. (*Pamela* does; *The Magic Mountain* doesn't.) Stories can be analysed, principles laid down. Who is this character? What does he want? How is he going to get it? Who, or what, stands in his way? Consciously or otherwise, every writer considers these questions when developing story ideas. But it's worth asking how far this can take us. I'd say: not far.

I wouldn't argue that novels shouldn't be planned. Some novelists plan extensively: Iris Murdoch, celebrated for the bizarrely convoluted plots of novels such as *A Severed Head* (1961), claimed to work out everything to the last detail before she set down a word. Agatha Christie went on long country walks to mull over the ins and outs of her detective puzzles. Other writers feel their way: E.M. Forster, when he began his masterpiece *A Passage to India* (1924), knew only that *something* would happen in the Marabar Caves.

Stephen King in *On Writing* (2000) notably disclaims advance planning.[6]

The question of whether to plan or not is an individual matter. What I'd say is that planning only comes into its own once a writer inhabits his or her particular world. In my view it's best to write something of the story, a certain amount of actual text, before thinking too much about where it's all going. Get to know the characters. Get to know the place. Approach a story externally, as an intellectual exercise, and you won't have the inwardness to make it come alive.

Structure emerges. It shouldn't be imposed.

Rules about how to write a novel, said D.H. Lawrence, are only good for novels that are copies of other novels.[7] E.M. Forster said something even better: that we learn how to write novels not by analysing them, but by enjoying them.[8]

Just as the reader goes to fiction for an experience of *immersion*, so the writer must first be immersed in the imaginary world. Whatever kind of book you're writing, that has to be true.

For more detail about how David creates the Storyworld of his own popular novels, turn to page 59.

Notes
[1] Somerset Maugham, *A Writer's Notebook* (Heinemann, 1949), p.246.
[2] There have been numerous critical studies of Richardson and his methods. Among the best are Margaret Anne Doody, *A Natural Passion: A Study of the Novels of Samuel Richardson* (Clarendon, 1974); Jocelyn Harris, *Samuel Richardson* (Cambridge University Press, 1987); and M. Kinkead-Weekes, *Samuel Richardson: Dramatic Novelist* (Methuen, 1973).
[3] See Robert Adams Day, *Told in Letters: Epistolary Fiction Before Richardson* (University of Michigan Press, 1966).
[4] The remark occurs in James' 1907 Preface to his 1879 novella *Daisy Miller*.
[5] See *Star Wars: The Annotated Screenplays*, ed. Laurent Bouzereau (Del Rey, 1997) for detailed information of the genesis of the script.
[6] See Peter J. Conradi, *Iris Murdoch: A Life* (HarperCollins, 2001), pp.431-3; Gwen Robyns, *The Mystery of Agatha Christie* (Doubleday, 1978), pp.189-90; E.M. Forster's 1953 *Paris Review* interview, available online at parisreview.com; Stephen King, *On Writing* (Hodder and Stoughton, 2000), pp.127-36.

[7] Letter to J.B. Pinker, 16 Dec., 1915. D.H. Lawrence, *Selected Literary Criticism*, ed. Anthony Beal (Mercury Books, 1961), p.20.

[8] Review of Clayton Hamilton's *Materials and Methods of Fiction* (1908); reprinted as Appendix to Abinger Edition of Forster's *Aspects of the Novel*, ed. Oliver Stallybrass (Edward Arnold, 1974), pp.138-9.

2

The Tale of Silly and Boring:
Matters Arising From a Simple
Storytelling Game

Philip Gross

A group of undergraduates are at work on storymaking theory. The fact that the course is on Writing For Children is incidental but it does give the lecturer, me, an excuse to sit down on the floor, cross-legged, and declare that for the next 15 minutes I'll be eight years old. Tell me a story, I say – out loud, one person at a time, with no pre-planning, simply picking up the thread and passing it on. To foil any urge for anyone to take control straight away, we start with one word at a time (including 'a' and 'the') but soon the game changes gear: each one can add a phrase, then a sentence, then one whole narrative step at a time. (What constitutes a *step* is a question in itself. It might be one word, or a paragraph, or even a well-staged telling silence.)

Every word of the content is theirs, but like any listening child with a responsive storyteller, I am not passive. I steer. Because I am not a particularly good polite child, the teller does not have to depend only on watching my eyes and my fidgeting. I am allowed to interject two words – "silly" or "boring". If the story seems to be tending to the predictable – if no fresh element has been brought into play for a few moves, or if the latest step is no more than logic would suggest, if there is no uncertainty: in short, if it's making *too much sense* – I will sigh a little, then say "boring".

On the other hand, if the invention is so fast and unrelenting that I start losing my grip on where we're going or on the logic of where we've come from, if the new occurrences aren't so much surprising as *so-what*, because, well, anything could happen so why care ... if there's *not enough* sense for me to want, fear or anticipate anything, then I'll frown. "Silly!" One word from me, bossy child, and the communal story, subtly, changes course. Somewhere down the fine line of balance between "silly" and "boring" is the sweet point of excitement, full attention, curiosity. Somewhere at the point of balance between total comfort (fine for lulling me to sleep, but it isn't a *story*) and total chaos (incomprehensible, by definition) is *adventure*. (If I'm very young, and it is really bedtime, the good story i.e. one that addresses my need, will lean towards comfort. At another age, when I need to prove myself with small ordeals, it will veer away.)

At any age, that line formed by the joined-up dots of sweet points will not be a straight one. Letting it waver a little to one side or the other for a while proves to be good style – letting it slow so the child on the floor is itching for the next leap, or giving a rush of surprise so that he's thinking "Hold on. What ...?" Both these reactions prove the point: we can rely on the listener to know how fast the story should be moving, and create little tensions by giving more or less. In either case, an appetite is roused, then satisfied, and so the story moves on.

The play-acting feel of this game, with everyone sitting in one circle and a listener as its hub, is more than just ice-breaking. It is creating a physical shape for the story – necessary because however much we can articulate the process theoretically it is something more physical – or physiological – that leads the storymaking in our heads or in a circle of listeners in the playground or the pub. We are sensing a level of arousal (or thwarting, or appetite) in ourselves and in the people we want to engage. We are a circuit. By putting the story shape out there around us in physical form, we can *think* about it less, yet be aware of it more. And isn't much of the work of stimulating writing about finding ways to be thoughtful, alert, intent ... without *thinking too hard*? (Here might lie the seeds of the conversation that the discipline of Creative Writing in universities has to have with itself, and with the institution round it. How do we rationalise the palpable need, acknowledged by most writers, for *intuition* – in other words, for *not* knowing too precisely or too soon what we are doing creatively, in academic terms?)

The circle shape says something else about the story. Though stories are commonly seen as things that move on – lines or journeys – much of their power derives from carrying with them the memory of where they have been – if not actually revisiting scenes then implying their presence as causes of subsequent events. (If not, the tale will be, literally, *inconsequential*.) In a storytelling circle we can see that what goes around comes around: we will be picking up and moving on material we have helped create. We are part of the history of the story, physically.

As the story tracks around the group, it becomes possible to sense the shape of it in the air between us. Here is a slow bit, where it lurks and idles. (Is this tedious, or teasing? How do we tell, or trust, the difference?) Here it jumps. (Has the new turn dropped out of nowhere, or has it been prepared for by the plot so far?) Or else we spot a loose end, a wild card of an idea introduced several moves ago – maybe as a desperate response to "Boring!" Nobody quite knows what the loose end means yet, or where it fits in the story. How long we can hold it in suspension depends in part on the age I, the listener, have decided to be, and whether I've chosen to accept an element of teasing as part of the game. But everyone recognises the sharp release and lift of the *Aha!* moment when it comes. The loose end not only weaves back into the story, but proves to have been absolutely necessary, the thing without which the story would have never reached its end. What this models for everyone concerned is the way that it might be the chance thought, or the eavesdropped comment, the whim that you have but can't justify while writing, that by forcing you to accommodate it leads you to a conclusion that you could not have pre-planned. Moral: don't discard too hastily the element that seems not to fit. (Children writing poetry, especially those who are 'good at writing', seem especially apt to discard misfitting elements – anything that seems to stand in the way of arriving at a finished product. Most writers-in-schools know the struggle to get young writers to preserve their drafts, to live with them for a while – denying themselves the satisfaction of crumpling them up, demonstrating tangibly that they've moved on.) A circle of people with differing ideas, needing to collaborate, can be a tangible image of Keats' Negative Capability – "when man is capable of being in uncertainties, mysteries, doubts, without any irritable reaching after fact and reason" (letter, 21.12.1817) – holding the uncertainty about where they are going until, palpably, the story clicks.

So the story moves around in a circle, but also (like a spiral) on through time. We can see what part of its life cycle the story seems to be in. Is it still introducing elements, pleasing me (the listening child) by moving an intriguing variety of pieces out onto the board? Is it pursuing its logic through the mid-game, starting to converge on the crunch that must come? (To go on throwing arbitrary new moves in at this stage could be both silly and boring, since what's engaging me now is the wish to see the story through.) Most groups seem to know when we've entered the final phase, when all the stray characters introduced have a limited time to reappear and prove themselves necessary. By Chekhov's dictum, the guns hung on the living room wall in Act One are going to have to be fired. It always impresses me how even competitive groups see, collectively, the point at which the ending needs to come, and applaud whoever comes up with the crisp last-liner. This must mean that by that point we have all become part of the self-feeding and self-pleasing organism of the story, and seeing it satisfy itself is more gratifying (while the game lasts) than our own small part in it.

"Silly" and "boring" – can words as blunt as this be building-blocks of narrative theory? They don't have the resonant clang of jargon coined from Greek roots (a manner commonly used by literary theorists to denote authority) – but maybe that is the point. If you want to know what story is, ask an eight-year-old. They have instincts. (I'm not using that word lightly. I'm suggesting that the forces that drive story may be physiological, hard-wired, even while every word or gesture they deploy derives from culture.) If your story doesn't work, an eight-year-old will know.

Too much sense ... too little ... If the 'comfort' extreme of the balance is a plenitude of sense – equilibrium, with no destabilising force, no inciting incident – what is its opposite? We could say not-sense – let's reserve the term Nonsense for that subtle and exquisite game, quite familiar to eight-year-olds, of which we'll say more later.

Better, maybe, to call it *not-yet-sense*, because the direction of a listener's listening is always towards making what sense they can of the elements offered to them. If they have accepted the mis-fitting things as irrevocably *not sense*, then they have started disengaging from the story. ("Silly," says the look in the listening child's eyes. Quick, you have a sentence or two in which to re-enlist them.)

But we're adults, aren't we? Academic readers especially, don't we pride ourselves on reading and relishing subversions, discontinuities, non-linear moves, open endings, unreliable narrators? But the game of the non-linear is that the reader's instincts will be struggling to pull the story into line, into one line or another, even as you say *Not that... Not that...* The game of unreliability is that the reader will try to know better, as surely as if they were reading an Agatha Christie. What is the classic pantomime moment, when every child in the house joins in? "*Be-HIND you!*"

How different is this, really, from the critic's dedication to deconstruct? Deconstruction, the deliberate over-reading of an author's intentions, is always the making of another, arguably higher meaning – discerning a pattern to which the writer was blind, but which our chosen analysis, our politics or ideology, reveals to us. The class struggle, the Freudian myth or the postcolonial struggle *becomes* the story.

Even Surrealism's challenge to sense, maybe the most dedicated on record, becomes a pleasure and a stimulation only when the reader or viewer has a sneaking sense of a connection, some underground tunnel that runs between things strangely juxtaposed. Not every odd meeting is Surreal. Some (to return to our young critic, sitting on the floor) are just silly. It is no accident that Nonsense verse invests so heavily in form, rhyme and logical structures – all the sounds that sense makes. "He thought he saw a Rattlesnake that questioned him in Greek./He looked again and saw it was the Middle of Next Week." In Lewis Carroll's 'Mad Gardener's Song', the frisson of this sideways leap – not just from thing to different thing but to a completely other sort of concept – is that what might be Silly is balanced precisely against the expectation (potentially Boring) that the second line and rhyme are going to explain the strangeness of the first away.

Only connect ... E.M. Forster's epigraph to *Howard's End* makes more than a literary point. On a fundamental, automatic level that is what brains are set to do: connect. Our circle of storymakers might already have demonstrated this, in what seems to be a light-hearted warm-up. In groups of any age, start a circle of word-associations round the group, and quite quickly you see several different ways in which our brains are wired to connect. Meaning, obviously ... but also rhyme and strong alliteration, or words commonly yoked together in a phrase, or in the same register of language. Stop the word-association game half way and change it to its opposite (say any word as long as it has no connection with the word before) and you see in practice how hard it is to evade the drift towards sense. (The best way to 'be good at' non-associations is to blank your mind to everybody else. It is also the least enjoyable, and least revealing. Playing this game to win is rather dull. Part of the participative pleasure comes from the laughter when someone else spots yet another connection of which the speaker is unaware.) Simple word association is a useful warm-up for a group, because everyone speaks and everyone can do it; it is a sovereign remedy for anyone who claims "I don't have any ideas", since having ideas is what our brains unstoppably do. (Preventing them takes twenty years of disciplined meditation.) But anti-associations tend to bring out frowns, near-panic and then sudden bursts of laughter. In particular, we see the moments when a chance juxtaposition brings a delighted "*Ah!*" from the group – the unfeignable visitation of the true Surreal, or (wearing its child-centred guise) true Nonsense.

Nonsense ... We might seem to have come on a long excursion from the idea of Story. The point, though, has been to push the dance of Silly and Boring, that inbuilt dialectic, to a telling extreme. (It is tempting to invoke yin and yang: pursue Silly to its fullness and you find a seed of Boring, and vice versa.) The important thing for new writers is that we can trust those opposite poles to be there when we read *and when we write.*

Collaborative games, like one-word-at-a-time stories, produce ideas because you are always encountering something that you had not planned in advance. Something, in fact, that *is not you.* (Confounding the distinction between self and other, and between writer and reader, might be one of the most useful experiences we can offer young creative writers. Learning to read the draft you have just penned as if it was by someone other is the fundamental insight we are training for in writing workshops, after all.) Being tangled up with the other might initially be a frustration to students whose idea of writing is self-expression. But it does not take much experiment to find that writing triggered by some unasked or random stimulus often comes out richer and more varied, and – in hindsight – *more* charged with glimpses of your own complex self than you could have planned in advance, with the ego firmly in charge. Being given the unasked-for word or image, and making the effort to hold it somehow in the same grasp as your own begins to look like a disciplined stretching exercise for Negative Capability.

Writing on our own, we have to find that unasked-for factor for ourselves. This might be a contradiction in terms, were it not for the fact that it tends to happen, almost in spite of ourselves, anyway. Many poems begin, experientially, with the *donnée*, the thing stumbled upon that feels *given*. Learning to value the unasked-for find, or the resistant material, or even the thought-provoking slip of a finger on the keyboard, is a skill learned in a grown-up writing life, and demands some confidence. The first irruption of that sense in my own work was 20 years ago, during a collaboration with another poet, Sylvia Kantaris, when she chanced to mention the title of a poem written by her son, at that time living in Colombia, 'The Air Mines Of Mistila' … Can I borrow that phrase, I asked, and write what I'm already seeing in it? Yes, I could. What I'd thought would be a playful homage to a nice turn of phrase took quite another turn when Sylvia read my poem and said "Yes, but where are the women in it?" Or rather, the next post brought a poem of hers, introducing the women of Mistila. And a story bred from there. (It is difficult to avoid the shade of Jung here: that meeting of male and female principles, animus and anima, did seem to *breed* – though as the work went on it grew harder and harder to tell which of us was writing for which gender. The book was published without names beneath the poems, so readers could try to guess who wrote which, and both writers were delighted when readers (generally) tried and got it wrong.)

In those first exchanges, Mistila seemed to be an exploration of a world, a wandering through a landscape, rather than a story. Neither of us was a novelist (then, that is – I write novels now, as well as poetry). But the sheer tendency for characters to imply back-stories and to generate wants and fears gave them *direction*. (Direction, that is, as in the momentum of a story, though it was also something like the role of a director in a film or play.) When characters met characters, there was a logic, contained in what we knew about them already, as to what they might do next. The proof of that came in later stages, as the poems bounced back and forth by first-class post. (This was before the days of e-mail, maybe fortunately.) More than once the two of us found ourselves imagining a character doing something, or imagining a whole new character, even, independently, in parallel. You could tell that as a spooky story, or as a New Age wonder-tale of writing channelled from beyond, but it is pretty clear to me that it was the characters themselves unfolding, with their inner logics and (the point of this excursion) their serendipitous elements and contradictions. The writing had started, unasked, with a found phrase. It went on with two writers' teasing resistance to each other's willed inventions, each throwing in elements designed to mis-fit with the other one's routines and habits of mind. At a certain point, the sum total of invention reached critical mass, and the inner logics started to create themselves. (Isn't the really validating moment in the writing of a novel when one of your characters turns round, looks you in the eye and tells you that *no way* are they going to do what your precious plot demands? Who do you think they are! Hard luck for the plot, but something more important has happened: in some real sense, the thing has come alive.) In the end, 'The Air Mines Of Mistila' was published as a 'verse fable' – admitting that it had become a story with a beginning, a middle ... And the last thing each of us wrote were cumulative bids towards an end.

Back in the circle of Silly and Boring everyone can sense the different movement that the piece has entered when we start conceiving that the next thing we say, or the one after that or after that, might be The End. The impulse to converge, rather than diverge, has the upper hand – the victory of Boring over Silly? It might be, were it not for the final balancing, which we reach experientially: the most satisfying end, the narrative punch-line, the clincher, is when the expected closure arrives, yes ... but arrives in a way that we didn't expect.

It might not be coincidence that I started writing my first novel not long after my sojourn in Mistila. Now I was storymaking solo, but I had learned to trust that sense of stumbling on something *other* in a story – something not quite planned or willed by me. The moment of palpable quickening in my writing of *The Song Of Gail And Fludd* was when two characters, shape-shifting, ambiguously-gendered jesters called Dumbgast and Flabberfound, wandered in as walk-on parts and, once on stage, refused to go away. At that point the plot I'd worked out in advance derailed, as Flabberfound and Dumbgast intervened, played tricks, laid traps and generally became the drivers of the story. In hindsight, these two were the paratroops of Silly, parachuted behind the lines of a story which had been conceived like a parable, with political and historical messages of which I was totally, Boringly, aware. I could scarcely explain to myself the thrill of adrenaline I felt when these anarchic characters would arbitrarily switch sides, stir things up, or create a terrible comeuppance for the just and the unjust, seemingly impartially.

Nor could I quite get over the disappointment when I tried to write a sequel to *The Song of Gail and Fludd*, and *instructed* the same characters to go and wreak their arbitrary misrule, on cue. And guess what, they were boring.

As I write this, my latest novel, *The Storm Garden*, has just appeared, and I notice how deep in its bones is a feeling of fascinated unease about the making of stories. The starting point, the given thing (*given* by a number of unrelated real-life encounters) is the character Max. This young man confesses to what appears to be a crime – a spectacular explosion at the opening of a shopping mall. But the apparent bombing turns out to have been an accident. Max, though, senses a story and steps into it. More worryingly, he has that quality essential for really thorough-going liars and hoaxsters (and I guess I should include creative writers) that on some level he *believes* that what he says is true. He is a fantasist, a 'pathological liar' in the sense that the stories he invents go way beyond any calculated plan or pay-off for himself. The current clinical label for his problem (or is it a gift?) is Narcissistic Personality Disorder. His disorder makes him horribly good at the job of lying. Even when Clio becomes embroiled with him, hoping at first to be the one to save him from himself, and the two of them end up on the run together, stumbling into deeper danger and crimes, no one can make up their minds

whether this is the story of two runaway teenage lovers, or a case of Stockholm Syndrome (the captive falls in irrational love with the captor) or a *folie à deux*. What interests me about the story is that I don't know, either. If I had known that, I might not have needed to write the book.

I could write a sound reflective piece, as many of our Creative Writing students do at our behest, about the narrative strategies I planned and employed in writing *The Storm Garden*. And it would be, sort of, true. But when I think back now, I mainly see myself as the listening reader (older than eight, to be sure, but still …) sat on the floor in the circle, in the whispering chamber of my skull. Each time there is a move to hustle Max into sense, into some mere diagnosis or some satisfying trauma in his early childhood that explains everything, that listener-me mutters *Boring*. Or every time Max does something too far off the edge of reason, then … *Silly?* – and Clio finds a necessary clue. And so the story moves on, and – if I know what's good for me – I follow.

3

Crabs (and stories) Walking Sideways: Life Beyond the Death of the Story

Andrew Melrose and Neil McCaw

This chapter is about the genesis of a novel for younger readers entitled *My Dad the Crab*. Along the way it is also about the death (and life) of the story form, about the relationship between critical baggage and creative spark(ing), and about the ways in which characters can (and should) take on lives of their own.

AM

It is part of my weekly routine to be sitting outside a music tutor's house in Brighton on a Friday evening. On one such evening I was listening to the radio while reading Paul Auster's *Oracle Nights* and I heard Mark Kermode, during one of his critical tirades on the state of modern cinema, and in particular *Ice Age 2*, commenting (that may have been complaining) on the death of narrative cinema. 'The death of narrative' was the part that got me thinking (though I share Kermode's view of *Ice Age 2* in this context). Narrative is story; it's a story of events and experiences; it's the process of telling a story; it's the part of the literary work that relates events; it is one of the truly multicultural givens in the world. "*Homo historia*, the history of our existence as a species is translated through stories, *homo fabula*, by our very nature we are a storytelling species who live, breathe, sleep and eat stories as part of the narrative of our very being."[1] How can it be dead?

Well, you might wonder what the story behind me was, sitting in my car, outside a music tutor's house. There may at some point be space to tell it, but in the meantime it is this idea of the 'death of narrative' that I want to pursue, even if it is hardly a new one.

Back in 1936, Walter Benjamin wrote:

> Familiar though his name may be to us, the storyteller in his living immediacy is by no means a present force. He has already become something remote from us and something that is getting even more distant. [2]

Benjamin's words were prophetic and to an extent I agree with them; this is only the emergent age of internet technology and already the parameters are expanding day by day. However, when Benjamin went on to say, " ... the art of storytelling is coming to an end ..." he entered a different debate, one that linked directly with the Kermode tirade I was listening to in my car that day. It is a debate I want to return to, but before I do I should tell you another story first.

Neil McCaw (**NM**) and I, Andrew Melrose (**AM**), both work at the University of Winchester where they have a number of Research Award initiatives, one of which is called the "promising researcher". The "promising researcher" initiative is a kind of buddy system, which allows either early-career academics to work towards getting their work published, or else mid-career academics to move beyond their normal field of expertise by teaming up with an established practitioner in another field to develop a project in this new field. I run the MA Writing for Children programme and have written numerous publications for children; Neil runs the BA Creative Writing programme, and is also an accomplished writer, but had never written for children before. We teamed up so that Neil could write a story for children. So (now I've given you the context) let's go back to the question of the 'death of narrative'.

Following on from Benjamin's prophecy on the death of storytelling, Jean Baudrillard argued that:

> ... the commodity form is the first great medium of the modern world. But the message that the objects deliver through it is already extremely simplified, and it is always the same: their exchange value. Thus at bottom the message already no longer

exists; it is the medium that imposes itself in its pure circulation. [3]

What is the 'message' if not the story? And, if Baudrillard was right (a big 'if', I know, but one that many have been persuaded by) were Neil and I about to embark on a fool's errand? Our shared and ongoing experience as literary critics, with longstanding critically theoretical credentials, seemed to point in that direction.

With some optimism amongst the pessimism I thought perhaps it could be reasoned that since the intended project was to be directed at children, this premonitory note from Baudrillard might not apply. After all, children's literature appears to be at an all-time high. But the well-known storytelling (for children) critic, Jack Zipes [4] wasn't convinced. In a book on the "troublesome success of children's literature" he wrote:

> In contemporary Western society we are not exactly suffering from a shortage of storytellers and stories. Every day we are inundated by one tale after another on TV and radio ... over the World Wide Web. But despite this deluge, something is missing ... we have lost the gift ... of using the power of story to share wisdom and build a meaningful sense of community.

It is a message which rolls Benjamin and Baudrillard's idea into one while still plying the 'death of narrative' tale. It is also one Zipes is keen to repeat, since much of his work is on the commodification of stories and the way they are used to hook children as consumers, and in particular to control their aesthetic interests and consumer tastes.

Of course, as critics, working broadly inside the discipline of English, Neil and I were well aware of the critical-theoretical position of such a debate. And yet we remained hopeful for our 'promising researcher' initiative.

Pretty soon I was able to get into my car without the Auster novel (which I greatly enjoyed), and instead to read what Neil had begun to write – of all things, a story.

NM

I must confess that I came to this project with a few doubts. For one thing, I was writing outside my comfort zone – this was the first time I had attempted to write fiction for children. For another, I had decided from the outset that I wanted one of my central characters to be a parent who was also a cancer sufferer, a subject with a very personal resonance for me. But my doubt went beyond these things. There was something else nagging away, and for the first weeks of the adventure that eventually became a novelette called *My Dad the Crab*, I wasn't entirely sure what it was; I just knew there was *something*.

The problem, I eventually realised, was with my background. My professional background, that is. Because since my adolescent experiments in the various forms a poem can take (or not), and those seemingly endless volumes of diary-form angst, much of what I had written before I started *My Dad the Crab*, was non-fictional. In particular, a fair proportion of it was literary-critical. There's been a novel for adults, on and off, to which I've returned at various points (only to abandon again), some biographies, a short film script, an exhibition, but the rest has been tightly argued theses on writers, periods, and themes. And the problem with this I've come to realise (amidst all the delights, for I honestly and truly love this writing) is that it gives you a particular view of the world. Most relevantly, for this project, it gives you a particular view of the nature of the story. You may try to resist, or argue to the contrary, but the bottom line is that those of us who spend most of our time writing 'lit-crit' can get bogged down, dare I say it, shackled, by some of its many assumptions about how literature works, and how stories are told/received/ interpreted. It doesn't *have* to be so, but it most often *is*.

This was my problem. Because whichever critical-theoretical perspective you write from, or even (as is the case with me) if you pretend that actually you don't have any particular partisan perspective, but instead absorb an array of different elements/aspects (just call me Mr Pastiche), it is almost inevitably the case that you absorb, by osmosis perhaps, a range of views about how stories/ narratives work. Or don't. And that is the issue; for there is something about literary-critical discourse that can't fail to make you suspicious of the 'good old yarn'. At an early stage, we critics are inducted into the wisdom of viewing anything that has a strong narrative with grave suspicion. Narratives, we are told, are means by which imperial ideology is enforced:

> ... the power to narrate, or to block other narratives from forming and emerging, is very important to culture and imperialism. [5]

Or else narratives are, by their very essence, about patriarchal domination – especially if they are linear; hence the work of critics such as Laura Mulvey, who have argued that 'distrust' of the linear narrative configuration is a key aspect of feminist revision. [6] The narrative form, we come to be suspicious of; we suspect that it most readily *prescribes* rather than *challenges* the status quo, that it maintains established political interests rather than subverting them. As the subtitle to Fredric Jameson's influential *The Political Unconscious* has it, narratives are always "socially symbolic acts". [7] Which leaves you feeling that in advocating a strong, crisp narrative form you do the literary equivalent of putting your hand up and admitting to be a racist/sexist/chauvinist, or (horror of horrors!) a liberal humanist; there is something in the ether that makes you feel as if you must deny the story, discredit it, tie a bell to it and shout "unclean".

This anxiety about the ideological implications of the narrative form is, I think, what lies behind the many (post)modern claims that the story is dead. There are no more good stories, apparently. We have lost the know-how necessary to tell a good tale. Rubbish. We may have become inhibited in our storytelling, or too anxious about the implications of our narratives, but that is not the same thing as there being nothing else to tell. Neither, as Christopher Booker would have us believe, [8] is it a case that there are no original stories left. The argument that all stories fit within one of a limited number of 'types' (rags to riches, quest, voyage and return, hero as monster, rebirth etc., etc.), is (to me, sorry) a depressingly reductive one. It's a bit like saying that modern football isn't exciting anymore because all the goals scored can be reduced to one of seven major types: the tap-in, the long-range shot, the header, the acrobatic goal, the own goal, the deflection, and the fluke. It smacks of the worst excesses of structuralism, which we have (thankfully) recovered from. It also smacks of a kind of fatalism that is the literary equivalent of Francis Fukayama's *The End of History*. Yes, I know that we are damn jolly clever these days, but does that *have* to mean that we yawn at everything?

So where was I? Ok, so once I had identified my postmodern angst about the death of the good old story, and started to work past it, I made a list of what I wanted *My Dad the Crab* to include. It was not a long list. I was clear from the beginning, for example, that I wanted my story to have a strong, multi-layered narrative arrangement. I had a theme (cancer). And I had a related image (a crab). The latter had come to me when I was reading about how in the US the sign of the zodiac that we know as Cancer is instead called The Crab. There seemed to be something appropriate about that, in a surreal sort of way; something confrontational, something I was slightly scared of. So with these things in mind I began to frame a few scenes, playing with my central idea. This soon became about 5000 words (some of which, I confess, I'd used more than once). And by this time I'd created a central character. He was a nine-year-old boy called Alex. And with the birth of Alex the tale at last began to come to life. He wasn't anything more than a shadow at this stage, but he was beginning to be interesting. Rather charmingly (I decided), and rather typically for a boy of his age (I knew from experience), he was oblivious to almost all of the really important things that were happening around him; and yet at the same time he was acutely aware of (and obsessed by) other, more trivial things.

So, with Alex bubbling away nicely, and with a skeleton of a plot, I had something to pass to Andy for comment. Which is what I did.

AM

Late on in his story about Tomas, the ghosted voice of Milan Kundera's narrator in *The Unbearable Lightness of Being* (1984), confesses to being the writer and staring back at his characters, back to when he first saw them as a shadow or a silhouette in the window, back to the point before he taught them how to speak, and I always found it to be a very affecting part of the novel. As I have written elsewhere:

> To witness a performance, read a book, watch a film, is to see the world presented anew. But to write such a story is to nurture

> the experience about to be presented and it is at this point that
> the authentic mark of the story must be stamped. [9]

Kundera was taking himself and his reader back to this point of his story, back to the point when it had barely started.

This relates directly to our early work on *My Dad the Crab*. With the half-sketched ideas, the shadow of Alex and a skeletal plot, I knew that for Neil this process was already underway. The authentic experience had already been encountered and nurtured and the story had begun. For all of Booker's storytelling reductionism, which Neil mentions above, rather than feeling like I was about to encounter another of those seven basic blessed plots, at the moment when I began reading about Alex I was immediately reminded of why I liked to read. It had nothing to do with critical analysis, theoretical positioning, academic rigour or reducing the story down to a basic plot, it was that once again I was about to see a world presented anew. For the time being that was enough for me to say "yes", we had a project. Thus, with 5000 words and a timetable ahead of us I had to begin to define a few guidelines so that the story could develop.

As this was someone else's story, I was mindful that I would have to consider the issues that sometimes I had begun to take for granted. This was my first consideration, what knowledge had to be passed on? The story was going to be for children, and having jumped through the 'death of narrative' hoop and dismissed it, the impossibility of children's fiction and the idea that it simply doesn't exist was another fairly well-trammelled idea we had to address. I won't reproduce the full debate here because it would take up too much space (it is summarised and can be traced back through Zipes, (2002), pp.61-80). But there is a point in my highlighting what I see as a couple of bookends to the argument.

In her book, *The Case of Peter Pan or The Impossibility of Children's Fiction* (1994), Jacqueline Rose writes:

> Children's fiction is impossible, not in the sense that it cannot be written (that would be nonsense), but in that it hangs on an impossibility, one which rarely speaks. This is the impossible relation between adult and child... Children's fiction sets up a world in which the adult comes first (author, maker, giver) and the child comes after (reader, product, receiver), but where neither of them enter the space in between. [10]

I really don't have much of a problem with most of this. When we refer to children's literature we are talking about literature written for children (and it must be *for*, never *at* or *to* if it is to retain the authentic experience of storytelling). What I do have a problem with is the idea that neither adult nor child can "enter the space … between". Surely the exercise here (one of literacy and writing for new readers) is for both the writer and the reader to reach into the "space in between": which exists only as experience. There is no binary opposition here between the author/receiver at each end of the space, as suggested by Rose. Children do not cross 'a space' to become adults, the gap is merely an ever-expanding experiential horizon. The child is latching onto the story and the storyteller's account of lived-out experience in an attempt to catch up, while the trace of continuing experience and historical memory is in constant development. As Adam Phillips (1995) argues:

> Children unavoidably treat their parents as though they were the experts on life … but children make demands on adults which adults don't know what to do with … once they learn to talk they create, and suffer, a certain unease about what they can do with words. Paradoxically, it is the adult's own currency – words – that reveal to them the limit of adult authority… Adults can nurture children … but they do not have the answers … *what they can do is tell children stories about the connections …* [11]

And this sums up the debate for me. The idea of nurture is a persuasive one. The so-called space between the child and the adult/writer is actually the place where the two collide, where the story exists, where experience and knowledge is nurtured and where real contact is made. Children do catch their parents/storytellers up (it is what growing up is all about – it is why the process is nurtured) and so in the meantime, on their catch-up journey the storyteller can only, " … tell children stories about the connections". So the issue becomes not 'why should we?' write for children but 'how?': To say 'story' articulates our existence, our essence, our very being as a thinking species, is a fact but it is no longer enough. It is necessary to understand it. [12] Neil was set the task of taking the story to the next stage: not lengthening, but THICKENING.

NM

One of the ironies of life is that sometimes your greatest strength is also your greatest weakness. That was certainly true of the initial draft of *My Dad the Crab*. I had spent a great deal of time creating Alex, my male, nine-year-old lead:

> My name is Alex Brian Wilson. I was named after a really old king I don't know anything about and a singer in a pop group called 'The Beach Boys' that my mum really likes. I was born on the 1st August, nine years ago. I am the youngest person in my year at school. I ALWAYS seem to be the youngest person in my year at school.

But in concentrating on *character* I had rather neglected *action*; I didn't even have a story framework with which to work out a plot; keeping the narratologist's distinction between *fabula* and *sjuzet* [13] in mind (one aspect of modern literary theory that I do find helpful in constructing fiction), it was pretty clear that I had neither.

Part of the reason I had focused on character so much was because (for me) all great stories, I mean *really* great stories, grow from characters. Heraclitus [14] was right (although completely inadvertently in this case), character is destiny; this is particularly so for the story. And I had known from an early stage that Alex needed to come to life before I could even think of doing anything with him. Most importantly, I had to get his voice right. Like Roddy Doyle does in *Paddy Clarke Ha! Ha! Ha!* I remember the first time I started reading that, and I just knew that the voice was true. And all my favourite novels, both for children and for adults, are driven by characters with voices, characters exhibiting the complexities, and frailties, and anxieties and hilarities of what it is to be a human being. When I was a child it was the Issy Noho books, and then those written by Roald Dahl – James and Charlie were my friends, I *knew* them. As an adult it's been Chandler (Marlowe), Eliot (Maggie Tulliver et al.) and Winterson (various). Stories driven by characters fuelled by real motivations and underpinned by psychological truth.

The problem was that I had created in Alex Wilson a character that resisted me every time I tried to impose a plot on him. Like one of those errant racehorses, backing away from the stalls as the handlers try with greater and greater exertions to force them in, Alex didn't want to climb trees, or ride his bike. He only wanted to write to himself in a notebook. And explore the world around him through his own ideas and questions. So after a short while I stopped trying to force him to do anything; I was that parent that shrugs his shoulders rather than committing himself to another twelve rounds of struggle. And at that point, *precisely* at that point, it just started to come. To flow. Alex got up off his bed and went downstairs to have his breakfast. I could see him, traipsing in the way that young boys do. He walked past the half-open door of the downstairs bathroom, and suddenly it happened. It was as if I was watching things unfold in front of me:

> Dad was in the bathroom. The door was slightly open and I could see the side of his face in the mirror.
> 'Morning Dad,' I said.
> 'Morning Alex,' he said.
> I went in to see him, because his voice was funny. Dad turned round. He had tears on his face. He had been crying. I was really surprised. I was sure it was only mums (and sometimes Nans) that cried. Not my Dad!
> 'Are you crying for no reason, or because you're sad ?' I asked.
> 'I've just got something in my eye,' he said.
> I didn't believe him. Perhaps he was crying about the same thing that Nan was crying about yesterday; although she had never told me what that was.

This was just the hook I had been looking for; my way in to the life of a boy who continually misreads the most obvious things in his life. A boy too busy uncovering so many other mysteries of his life that he fails to realise that there is a huge mystery, a potentially earth-shattering mystery, right in front of him. Because Alex (and I had made my mind up about this right at the outset) has a Dad who is suffering from cancer. And the story of Alex (which, because of the way his mind works, serves as a sub-plot even though in reality it is *the* plot of the novel as a whole) is the story of a family who are in their different ways sharing the trauma of cancer. And the layering of the narrative comes because half the members of the family (i.e. the children) don't even know what cancer is.

One of the best pieces of advice Andy gave me about that first draft was that I needed to give Alex an outlet. He was too much of a loner, he didn't have anyone to confide in. I had thought that it would be possible to handle this through the use of diaries, with discrete entries being included as whole chapters, but Andy convinced me that that this wasn't enough. It didn't get Alex 'out there', and he was too isolated from the world outside. Andy suggested that I might want to develop the personalities of Alex's friends, to give him some counterpoint.

I took this on board. First of all, I found a role for Alex's best friend, Peter. Having said that, to say I 'found' a role for him is perhaps a little disingenuous. In truth it was Alex who found the role for him; Alex the discoverer of mysteries, the amateur sleuth, needed a companion. An ear. A WATSON! Like all detectives, big and small, what Alex most needed in the world was a trusted friend who worked as both confidant and sounding-board alike. As such, Peter came into being.

This happened just at the moment when something else occurred. Alex's little brother, Billy, who in the earliest draft had been no more than a solitary mention, started his own journey towards life. As part of the job of 'thickening' the narrative I had initially added a few other references to him, but it wasn't until his first real scene, the first occasion on which the reader is allowed to see his personality, that I became aware of his rich potential. I created a scene where Billy puts on his Dad's oversize coat and entertains his mother and brother with a comic impersonation, and at a stroke he had developed a *personality*. A life of his own. Andy was taken with the character of Billy straight away. He insisted I give him more lines and more to do in the next rewrite.

AM
When asked recently to name a favourite children's book my immediate response was *Holes* by Louis Sachar. If I had taken time to reflect I might have made a different choice but what struck me about *Holes* was the way in which Sachar not only explored the experiential plot flanked by the adult and the child (as I've discussed above), but also the way in which the novel itself reached into that territory, exploring a view of the world as seen by children and adults, where the two have to meet. One of the things that makes this novel more successful than others is the way the secondary characters help

to pull (or that might be push) the story along.

In *My Dad the Crab*, the introduction of Alex's best friend Peter was, for me, inevitable; the story couldn't survive without him. Along with Peter came some of the story thickening. We managed to see Alex outside the home environment, out into the world of knowing for a child, in this case school and all the other distractions that followed. It also enabled the introduction of a sub-plot, the case of the ghosts in the girls' toilets, which added to the 'mystery' element of the piece and helped to round Alex's character as someone who really did like to uncover and to solve. Yet, even with Peter and a nice sub-plot supporting the main story there was something missing; the story still wasn't located centrally enough, there was still a gap between the 'Dad' story and Alex solving the mystery. It was like the stories were going down two strands of railway track, both going in the same direction but the Dad narrative on one track and the Alex narrative on the other, with nothing holding them together – in fact the mystery was keeping them apart. And then something magical happened.

As Neil has already said, Billy arrived:

> Billy came into the room. He had one of Dad's jackets on.
> 'Hello, I'm Dad,' he said, in a loud deep voice. Mum and I laughed. She gave me another squeeze.
> 'I'm just going to fix the washing machine,' Billy continued. He picked up his plastic sword, which was on the table. He walked over to the washing machine and started hitting it furiously.
> 'There, that's better,' he said. Mum and I laughed some more.

If Alex and Dad were the heroes holding the piece together, Billy became the heart and soul of it. In his even more innocent youthfulness (as the little brother) Billy didn't need any of the rationalising thoughts of Alex, or Dad (and any of the other adult characters who drifted in an out). Billy could say the unsayable and do the undoable ('out of the mouths of babes' is less of a cliché and more of a truism). Thus Billy's entrance as Dad, wearing his jacket and 'unfixing' the washing machine suddenly brought the whole family (and the story) into view; now it was real, Alex's abstract musing on the 'mystery' and the adults skipping round the subject of cancer were all brought into focus by Billy who said what everyone was avoiding: they all missed Dad and he missed them.

How was it magical? Well it came out of nowhere, it was like the character was writing his own voice in the story. Hitherto relegated to a bit part, it was as if Billy had decided it was time to speak up. Of course, to dress Billy in his Dad's jacket as a means of delivering the message was also a magical moment (and one that stuck out in my mind) because the whole psychology of the moment was true; wrapped up in the imaginative idea of a child and childhood, do we not all have stories about our own dressing up? In storytelling terms, as Freud reminds us:

> Should we not look for traces of imaginative activity as early as in childhood …? Might we not say that every child at play behaves like a creative writer, in that he creates a world of his own, or, rather, rearranges the things of his world in a new way, which pleases him. It would be wrong to think he does not take life seriously and he expends large amounts of emotion on it … The creative writer does the same as a child at play. He creates a world of fantasy which he takes very seriously – that is, which he invests with large amounts of emotion – while separating it sharply from reality. *Language has preserved this relationship between children's play and poetic creation* [my italics]. [15]

A simple rationale really, but in real terms Billy's late entrance into the story (in Chapter 31) allowed Neil to go back and re-introduce him and develop his take on the proceedings, nurturing the relationship between "children's play and poetic creation". How can story be reduced to a basic commodity-driven plot when the magic that is the human story overtakes all other considerations to find itself space to be told ? "Hello, I'm Dad," he had said.

NM
It's strange really, because in some ways I had travelled in an almost complete circle. I'd begun the writing project too tight with critical-theoretical angst, too bogged down in the impossibilities of the story and a suspicion of the narrative form. Then I'd managed to work

around those things, given life to characters (who had then written their own scenes), and started to piece together the patchwork that was becoming *My Dad the Crab*. Alex's story was one of constant revelation, in which the hierarchy between the trivial and the consequential had become inverted, and the various plots and sub-plots combined to produce a tale with multiple layers and concerns. Most importantly, for me, it had become a novel about cancer which wasn't about cancer at all; which had been my most cherished aspiration right from the beginning. And then (hence the point about me coming full circle), at the conclusion of what must have been the third or fourth draft, I found that the critical-theoretical notions that had initially inhibited me were now empowering me and my understanding of how the narrative hung together.

For the truth of it was that my two lead characters, Alex and Billy, although quite inadvertently and unwittingly so on my part, were embodiments of a broadly Lacanian [16] sense of childhood development. Billy lived in an *imaginary* realm, pre-existing the "transformation that takes place in the subject when he assumes an image".[17] True, Billy's experience of the imaginary fell outside the strict Lacanian sense of the term (he was a little too old), but nevertheless he resided in a place where (for children) they *are* the world, they are inseparable from it, and as such (quite often) are completely unseeing in terms of its questions and anxieties. He had evolved as a counterpoint to the lead character of Alex who, on the other hand, was of the *symbolic* world, where language (writing, reading, talking) had become central, a character busy trying to negotiate himself around that world. He was the one rationalising everything around him, and one of the charms of the story was (I hoped) the idiosyncratic way in which he was doing so. For Billy life was something far more instinctive, primal even. He was the id, uncontrolled and restricted by the world and its tediousness, delighting in unlimited possibilities and unregulated behaviours. Alex was much closer to the ego, more regulated, even if ultimately working outside these regulations as much as he could. Together, they implied the development of the child towards a growing consciousness and an immersion into the world of words and representations.

It is in the conjunction of these two child selves, Alex and Billy, that the story of *My Dad the Crab* comes to life. At its core, and most simply, *My Dad the Crab* is a story about the personality of two boys; boys who are both commonplace and extraordinary. Boys who, when viewed together, pretty much represent *all* boys, and the glorious way they trip and stumble through life. It is born of a fascination with their characters and their oh-so-human eccentricities, enacting, over all of its chapters, the uncanny ways in which they perform (Billy), and read (Alex), the world around them.

It was only when I had finished writing that I realised that *My Dad the Crab* had become a story about stories. The reader encounters a series of stories within a story which itself lives inside the body of (yet) another story (like a kind of infinite regression). Further, each of the strands of the narrative not only invites the reader to decode the events and to achieve their own satisfaction by understanding them, *they are reliant on this happening*. The reader is an integral, valued part of the development of the narrative(s). As such, in its own humble little way, *My Dad the Crab* tries to operate like the classics of children's literature that I so adored as a child. Because for me, novels such as *Swallows and Amazons*, *Huckleberry Finn*, *The Wind in the Willows*, and *Danny, Champion of the World* worked because of how they made me *feel*; they made me feel engaged, sure, and ultimately satisfied, but not before (and most importantly) they had made me feel as if I *belonged*. The joy of the story form is the moment when it pauses to put an arm around your shoulder and to reassure you that you are part of it all: indeed, is this not the biggest contributing factor in the enduring success of *Harry Potter* – where the alienation of Harry, Ron and Hermione reaches out to every child? When reading novels as a child I was a privileged insider, one of the gang, a key element of the story. And this is the promise that the best children's fiction must hold open; that the child-reader is crucial to the unfolding drama. Great writers capitalise on our innate sense of wanting to be part of things, of wanting to join in. Of wanting to *belong*.

AM

So anyway, there I was, sitting outside this music tutor's house in Brighton, waiting for my daughter's lesson to end, when this huge monster rose out of the sea …

NM

And so the story is dead ? Tell me another one.

Notes

[1] Andrew Melrose, *Storykeeping: The Story, the Child and the Word in Cultural Crisis* (Paternoster, 2002), p.3.

[2] Walter Benjamin, *Illuminations*, trans. Harry Zohn, ed. With an introduction by Hannah Arendt (Fontana, 1973), p.83.

[3] Jean Baudrillard, 'The Ecstasy of Communication', Hal Foster, ed., *Postmodern Culture* (Pluto Press, 1985), p.131.

4 Jack Zipes, *Sticks and Stones: The Troublesome Success of Children's Literature from* Slovenly Peter *to* Harry Potter (Routledge, 2002), p.127.

[5] Edward Said, *Culture and Imperialism* (Vintage, 1994), p. xiii.

[6] Laura Mulvey, 'Changes: Thoughts on Myth, Narrative and Historical Experience', *History Workshop*, 1. 23 (Spring 1987), pp.3-19.

[7] Fredric Jameson, *The Political Unconscious: Narrative as a Socially Symbolic Act* (Routledge, 2000).

[8] Christopher Booker, *The Seven Basic Plots: Why We Tell Stories* (Continuum, 2004).

[9] Andrew Melrose, *Write for Children* (Routledge, 2002), pp.21-22.

[10] Jacqueline Rose, *The Case of Peter Pan or The Impossibility of Children's Fiction*, revised edition, (MacMillan, 1994), pp.1-2.

[11] Adam Phillips, *Terrors and Experts*, (Faber, 1995), pp.1-2.

[12] Andrew Melrose, *Storykeeping: The Story, the Child and the Word in Cultural Crisis* (Paternoster, 2002), p.13.

[13] Put simply, this is the distinction between the 'story' (the broad frame of events) and the 'plot' (the narrative arrangement/treatment of those events).

[14] Heraclitus, the Greek philosopher (c. 6th century BC).

[15] Sigmund Freud, *Art and Literature* (Penguin,1990), pp.131-2).

[16] Paralleling concepts first articulated by the psychoanalyst Jacques Lacan (1901-1981).

[17] Jacques Lacan, 'The Mirror Stage as Formative of the Function of the I as Revealed in Psychoanalytic Experience', in Philip Rice & Patricia Waugh eds., *Modern Literary Theory: A Reader* (Edward Arnold, 1992), p.123.

4

Making Versions:
A Storytelling Journey with *Ramayana*

Sally Pomme Clayton

Through blue heaven
flew Garuda, king of the birds
carrying Gods Vishnu and Lakshmi on his back.

As I flew over the sea between Kerala and Sri Lanka, dawn broke, and the sky and sea merged in radiant blue. For a moment I imagined I was flying on Garuda's back. I thought of the characters in *Ramayana* who had crossed the stretch of water between India and Lanka, the Demon Kingdom: Sita kidnapped by Ravana; Hanuman, Monkey God, who leapt across the sea to find her; Rama and his brother Lakshman who waged war for her.

During 2004 I collaborated with director Tony Graham, The Unicorn Children's Theatre, and a band of Indian musicians to create a performance for young audiences of the Indian epic, *Ramayana*. In between rehearsals I travelled to Sri Lanka to see the landscape the story inhabits. As the plane descended through puffs of cloud, an idea floated into my mind. My trip was to last 18 days – I swiftly divided the story into 18 sections – I would think about one section each day, meditate on it, look at my surroundings through it, and carry the story with me as I travelled.

I had been telling traditional stories for over twenty years, and should have been more careful about embarking on this idea. I knew stories had their own reality. Whenever I told a particular fairytale about a fox, I would see a fox dashing past me after the performance. Weather responds to stories. During the first performance about mysterious goddess Lilith, as I spoke Lilith's name, there was a huge crack of thunder. When telling a Russian fairytale, as I introduced the witch Babayaga, there was a flash of lightening. I knew that a story is never just a story, yet didn't think about the implications of what I was going to do. Not only did I meet the story, I found myself living inside it. It could all just be coincidence, but isn't coincidence the realm of myth?

Multiple versions

Vishnu and Lakshmi looked down on Earth,
and saw demons.
'Demons are taking over the world,' said Vishnu.
'We must go down to Earth and stop them.'

Vishnu and Lakshmi incarnate as Rama and Sita, and *Ramayana* begins. The epic has been performed throughout India and South East Asia for at least 2000 years. The earliest text dates from 400 AD, written by the poet Valmiki, who brought together stories and songs connected to Rama and Sita in 25,000 metric verses. There are countless other versions of the epic throughout India and South Asia. Some notable ones are the 11th-century Tamil version by Kamban etched on palm leaves. And the 16th-century *Ramacharita manasa* by north Indian poet Tulsi Das. The versions of Valmiki and Tulsi Das have become classic texts. But these texts don't end with the page – *Ramayana* was, and is, a living oral tradition. Even today, stories connected to *Ramayana* have not been written down. [1]

The epic's origins are in India and Hinduism, but the story has crossed seas and mountains, languages and religions, performance styles and art forms. There are Muslim versions in Java and Buddhist versions in Thailand. The story exists as shadow plays in Indonesia and temple carvings in Cambodia, and in myriad forms of enactment throughout India. The written *Ramayana* texts are versions, and the performances are versions too, that create and re-create the written texts, making endless new versions. Any one of these versions is huge. *Ramayana* is made up of episodes and episodes, sub-stories and side-stories. Each character has a back-story, which has back-stories and side-stories. *Ramayana* is a narrative with no ending.

When I first started telling traditional stories I thought I could find the oldest, purest version of a story, but soon discovered my research was not a linear thread leading back to an original 'Ur-text'. Instead it was a tangled mass of threads – of stories, leading to stories, leading to stories. The story threads moved backwards and forwards through time, across linguistic and geographic boundaries, incorporating oral and written influences. In the end there is no 'Ur-text', just versions, of versions, of versions. Each storyteller engages in the creative process of making their own version.

Ramayana can be told for weeks and weeks and still not be finished – my version was to last 90 minutes! In India *Ramayana* is not told in a linear way, certain sections are repeatedly enacted, but the audience know the whole story and missing episodes are filled out by the culture that surrounds the story. I read many versions of *Ramayana*, comparing comic strips with sculptures, classic texts with TV dramas, puppet shows with poems. Variations and versions got jotted down in notebooks, then I made my own line through the narrative. As I worked on my version I imagined an audience who would know little about the story, I wanted to give them the drama of the whole narrative, even though it would mean chopping out vast amounts of story.

During rehearsals the musicians [2] would often stop to tell me stories I had omitted. Sometimes I knew the story, but mostly I had not come across their tales which existed in oral form, outside the corpus of classic texts, often connected to the religious practices that surround *Ramayana*. We discussed the implications of my choices, and I gained insights into the beliefs encircling the epic. My perceptions of characters altered, in particular of Demon King, Ravana. The musicians did not see him as evil, but rather as a god, whose purpose is to allow Rama to fulfill the destiny of killing him.

Story in the landscape
As I travelled through Sri Lanka I meditated on a section of the story each day and found *Ramayana* imprints everywhere. I visited Ravana's Waterfall, passed tea estates named for Sita, and saw a gleaming truck named for Rama's brother: 'Lakshman motor horse'

35

inscribed above the window. I visited Sri Lanka before the tsunami, in a period of relative calm. The island is densely populated but fertile, and even in the dry zone resourceful communities manage to grow crops. Many families are involved in small industries based on knowledge passed down for generations. Sri Lanka still struggles to recover from the devastation left by the tsunami. But living in this demanding climate, Sri Lankan people have always been inventive, and the character of the people, and inexhaustible fertility of the island, brings hope for the future.

I began to find parallels between the section of the story I was working on, and that day's events. As I was thinking about Sita's wedding celebrations of music and processions, I rode an elephant, then spent the evening with musicians who had a huge repertoire of devotional songs – *bhajans* – about Rama and Sita. The musicians asked me to tell some *Ramayana*. I told Sita's birth, and they improvised around it, underlining my speech with tabla rhythms. Afterwards they said, "*Ramayana* dance-drama used to be popular, but it's not performed so often now." Then they laughed. "We prefer techno," they said.

Familiar patterns – unique combinations

Traditional stories consist of narrative patterns and images that appear and reappear over and over again. [3] For example, Sita's capture by Ravana has elements of the 'Snow White' type fairytale: an innocent girl is tempted out of safety by evil-doer in disguise. Rama enacts the fallen hero pattern found in Greek myths such as *Jason and the Argonauts*: the hero is about to achieve his goal, but a flaw in his character undermines him. Structural patterns like these have survived history and seem to be eternal, yet a storyteller's route through these patterns is never entirely fixed. The opportunities for re-combining these patterns are endless, giving the teller freedom to make the tale theirs. [4] Working with these patterns, a storyteller learns how to: create anticipation and suspense; find the drama in repetition; incorporate dialogue and use asides. [5] Ultimately the flexibility of traditional tales offers storytellers the possibility of saying something unique, of making something new out of familiar material. It is what the teller does with the patterns that is interesting, and distinguishes one teller from another. The survival of a tale depends on this process, allowing the story to keep coming back in different forms.

Meeting the story

For part of my trip I joined a group led by a local guide, and made friends with artist Jess. Early one morning, we visited Sigiriya, a 5th-century palace built on a massive rock rising 200m out of the surrounding plain. This fantastic construction was built by King Kasyapa who killed his father in a demonic rage, then built the fortress to protect himself. On top of the rock is a marble dance floor where Kasyapa would watch 50 maidens dancing. Strangely, Kasyapa did not stay in the security of the fortress he had built, but went out to defend his palace on the back of an elephant, and died in the jungle. It is said that the dancing maidens were so grief-stricken they hurled themselves from the top of the rock to their deaths. Fact merges with fiction, making the story richer. The emotional resonances of history echo in the imagined stories that spring from it – both containing their own truths.

Something similar was happening to me, as the story, my imagination, and my experiences seemed to merge. Both Jess and I had begun to feel awkward when our guide placed too frequent helping hands on our backs and arms. As we climbed Sigiriya, the group forged ahead and I got left behind. Our guide came to help me, and as I clung to the rails of an ancient spiral staircase that hung dizzily from the rock face, I grappled with feelings of distaste and politeness towards him. I imagined how Sita must have felt when Ravana captured her, brought her to Lanka, and tried to impress her with his palace. And how Sita, not wanting to be his queen, became his prisoner.

After a night of drinking arrak – fermented palm sap alcohol – our guide drunkenly forced his way into both mine, and Jess', rooms. I felt I had met an aspect of Ravana. And my thoughts turned to the rest of the story – there were war and battles, deaths and fire, to come. How would these episodes manifest? Why hadn't I thought of this before I started? But it did not feel possible to stop. I had to keep going until I reached the end.

Visualisation

Once I have worked out the structure of the story, I visualise the narrative in my mind's eye. This is when the story comes alive. Through visualisation I see the logic and consequence of narrative events, which helps me resolve problems with the story. It also reveals the humour of a situation, or the comedy of a character's actions, and I spontaneously find jokes. Visualisation is not just about seeing images, it involves all the senses – from conjuring temperature and texture, to hearing characters' voices. I visualise the story from each character's viewpoint – this helps create a multi-dimensional perspective rather than a simple moralistic message.

Telling a story is not about repeating a learned script, it is like jazz, an improvisation around a theme. In performance the process of visualising supports the memory, helping guide the teller through the plot, from image to image, rather than word to word. Tellers usually have some memorized sections and phrases, these are often more poetic, and in some traditions have been handed-down from teller to teller. [6] My *Ramayana* combined freer sections, with memorized phrases that I wanted to speak at specific points. For example, the phrase "remember who you are" was repeated during my telling, spoken by different characters at different moments, gathering and changing its meaning through the narrative.

The experience of listening to images rather than a learned script is different. Strong visualisation on the part of the teller creates the impression in the listener that the tale is true. The story seems to exist, not as words passing through the teller's mind, but as lived fact. The tale seems to come from the bodily experience of the teller, and this has a different effect on the listener. The natural response of a child when they have heard a tale told in this way, is to ask, "is it true?" The images are physically embodied by the storyteller through eyes and intonation, gesture and movement, rhythm and silences. The physicality of storytelling allows images to be transmitted even when a story is being told in a language foreign to the listener. [7] Another layer is added to the visualisation by the listener, as they enact the story in their imagination, casting it with people and situations that are close to them, filling the story with their own experiences, values and memories. Visualisation is the deep experience of storytelling, and is what leads listeners to express the feeling of being transported somewhere else.

Story contexts

On the site where Ravana imprisoned Sita, is a Hindu temple, Sita Amman Kovil. A driver took me to the shade of a lush mountain and I found *Ramayana* alive. Painted scenes of the story cover the temple walls, and there are shrines to Rama, Sita and Hanuman. Beside the temple is a large rock embedded with giant footprints – the footprints of Hanuman as he jumped to Lanka, found Sita imprisoned here, and gave her Rama's ring.

I wanted to do a *puja* – a blessing – for my performance. My driver was a Christian, but knew what I needed to do. He took me to a shop where they made an offering for me, arranging fruits, flowers, camphor, and incense. A radiant priest took my offering and touched the fruit to the lips of the Rama and Sita statues, feeding the gods of the story. The priest sang a prayer and rested a shining gold helmet on my head – momentarily I was imbued with Rama's spirit. The ritual was repeated at the Hanuman shrine. Then the camphor was set alight, and I walked round the temple three times, thinking of all the fires in the story. *Ramayana* is not a story, but a religious mystery that you can participate in directly.

Around the temple the earth is very black, said to have been burnt black when Ravana caught Hanuman and set fire to his tail. This black earth has been excellent for growing tea ever since! Hanuman escaped, returning to Lanka with Rama and his army. War begins, and Lakshman is wounded. Hanuman, ever faithful, flies to the Himalayas to fetch a magic herb from the Medicine Mountain to heal Lakshman. But Hanuman finds the mountain covered in herbs and he does not know which is the right herb.

> *Hanuman placed the mountain on the palm of his hand*
> *and flew back to Lanka.*
> *'I didn't know which herb to pick,' he said.*
> *'So I brought the whole mountain.'*

The lush mountain looming behind Sita's temple is said to be the very mountain Hanuman brought back from the Himalayas. On its slopes are Hakgala Gardens growing rare herbs used for the tonics of Ayurvedic medicine. Reality, history and fiction had merged, and I had fused with them. All the time my driver stood beside me, partaking in every aspect of the ritual. Like me, this was not his religion, but unlike me, he knew all the gestures and the prayers as if they were his own. As we left the temple, my driver nodded. "It makes your heart calm," he said.

The musicians were rooted in the living dialogue that surrounds this story. During rehearsals, I brought in a knitted toy monkey, and he was given the part of Hanuman! We explored ways I could make the monkey speak and move. When Hanuman carries the medicine mountain – the toy monkey wrapped his arms around me and carried me across the stage – through Tony's direction the illusion looked convincing. When Ravana catches Hanuman – I held the monkey high and dropped him. The musicians said, "We don't like Lord Hanuman being dropped. Hanuman is a God. He should not be dropped." Tony and I weakly argued it was "a theatrical device". But the musicians disagreed, for them the monkey was not a toy or a puppet, he was imbued with power. I found it hard to accept that we had to sacrifice this theatrical moment because my scruffy monkey was too god-like to perform it. The next day Tony decided we would not drop the monkey. And it was a turning point for me. I glimpsed the story from the perspective of living inside it.

Listeners

When *Ramayana* is told in Northern India, a white cloth is spread for Hanuman to come and sit on, and listen to the story. It is said that whenever *Ramayana* is told, Hanuman is always there, listening, "the first to arrive and the last to leave". The listener plays a vital part in making the story. His or her responses inspire and change the performance. Timing, jokes, dialogue, structure … are continually shaped through a live audience. In a sense, it is the listener who creates the tale. This process of repeated telling and listening is what makes a version. The repetition can create a 'text', as phrases are formed and refined. But as the audience is always new, the storyteller is always adapting the 'text', making large and small shifts to words, structure, and images, in response to the changing surroundings. The experience, and the 'text', is never the same twice. So even though a story might have been told hundreds of times, it is happening once, and never again.

Gods and Demons

The battle raged.
Demons loosed arrows and wielded knives.
Rama's army fought back, hurling rocks and trees.

I had arrived at the darkest section of the epic – the war. And in the boiling midday sun I bumped into the festival of Skanda – God of War. Skanda has always been popular in Sri Lanka and is depicted with six heads and twelve hands each holding a different weapon. I had seen images of Skanda in both Hindu and Buddhist temples. Presented beside Buddha, the God of War appeared peaceful; Skanda's weapons seemed devotional objects to slay ignorance and kill demonic aspects of the mind. With a deafening clash of drums, a cart rolled past. Hanging from the cart was a boy with huge metal hooks piercing the flesh on his back and shoulders, pulling fiercely at his skin. More hooks were attached to his arms, legs and cheeks. His eyes were empty, as if in a trance. "What is it?" I asked Jess. "It's an honour," she whispered. What looked like pain and suffering, was devotion and sacrifice, maybe even ecstasy.

The idea that, by acknowledging the dark side its power is reversed, runs through Sri Lankan culture. Demons are understood differently, they are guardian deities, agents of health and well-being. Demon masks are placed in newly-built houses to protect them. A *devil dance* is performed to heal disease, where masked dancers honour the demon of the disease by dancing all night. I wanted my version of *Ramayana* to convey a sense of this paradox. I portrayed Ravana as dignified and powerful, rather than evil. And described the battle scenes from both the demons' and the gods' viewpoints, showing how loss and gain is the same for both sides.

Saying goodbye to Jess, I made my way to Ambalangoda, to the museum of masks. New masks were displayed alongside priceless treasures portraying cobra demons, mermaids, and kings. [8] I bought a demon puppet with fangs and a sword, and was told, "It's a house demon, he will protect your home". I found a small guesthouse to stay in, and met a graceful old man sitting on the veranda. "This is Mr Chitrasena," said my host. "The greatest storyteller in Sri Lanka." Mr Chitrasena had a face I can only describe as a mask – emotions, thoughts and memories seemed to hang and move across his features.

He was a famous dancer and his work explored all forms of dance, innovatively combining traditional Indian and Sri Lankan dance with contemporary forms. He had enacted all the myths, and said one of his favourite characters was Ravana. He showed the rolling-eye movements that define Ravana, and the bow and arrow gesture that belongs to Rama. And spoke of *rasa* [9] – the shared experience, or flavour, that passes between artist and audience. [10] He inspired me to explore stylized gesture in my performance, and during the war sequence I mirrored the experiences of Rama and Ravana by giving them identical gestures and dialogue. [11] That night I heard drumming. It continued until dawn, the heavy, pounding, rhythm of a *devil dance*. It was trance music, and it entered my mind and dreams, so that I too felt I had been healed.

I had passed the worst bit of the story now – meeting Ravana had not been so bad. When the war is won and Ravana dead, Rama is reunited with Sita. But Rama does not behave like a god. He is overcome with jealousy, and behaves like a human being, or a demon. Rama is convinced Sita has betrayed him, and Sita outraged, proves her innocence by walking through fire.

> Sita walked through the flames
> and not a thread on her dress caught fire.
> And as she walked, the flames turned to flowers.

Sita is an underlying figure in people's beliefs and cultural practices, especially in the ritual of 'Treading the flowers'. I witnessed two dancers praying before a shrine to Lakshmi, then stepping with bare feet onto a tray of burning coals. The dancers took sturdy steps into the fire, walking through leaping flames, treading the flowers. The dancers prayed to Lakshmi as they walked. Lakshmi is, of course, the goddess who incarnates as Sita. And like Sita, the dancers' courage and faith to tread the flowers protects and transforms them.

A Listening Universe
Rama and Sita follow a trail of lights home to India. This moment is celebrated by Hindus as Divali – the festival of lights. The trail has travelled all over the world, and diverse communities now enjoy Divali. I made my way home, and when I arrived found my car missing and the front door unlocked. As I pushed open the door, I

saw clothes and papers tumbling down the stairs. I had been burgled. My flat had been turned upside-down, and anything valuable driven away. It was hard to accept the burglary was just coincidence. The story seemed an energetic force with its own reality. The musicians believe this reality, and said, "You visited Ravana's house – so he came to visit yours. Why didn't you go to Rama's [12] house?" When I was brave enough to move back home, I hung the demon with his sword by the front door.

I felt I had met *Ramayana* directly. And the story had warned me, reminding me that a story is not just a story, that stories exist in a listening universe, a universe that responds to thought and dream, a universe of correspondences. Perhaps the imaginative process of bringing a story to life is not so different from working on a novel? Except an oral story is in a continual process of becoming. Unlike written stories, final versions of oral performances are never made. Orality is a never-ending process that continually influences the tale. The power of traditional stories lies in this adaptability. New versions can reflect current events, connect past with future, and make meanings out of present experience. This flexibility allows *Ramayana* to continue its endless journey. [13]

Notes

[1] The fluid and interconnected relationship between written and performed versions of *Ramayana* has been documented in Paula Richman's (1991 and 2001) excellent collections of essays.

[2] The musicians were: Ajit Pandaye from Ahmedabad – tabla; Sukhdev Mishra from Varanasi – violin; Shyan from the UK – Bansuri – flute; Rick Wilson from the UK – percussion, electronic composition, and musical director. Creating the show was a collaborative act between all the artists and the director.

[3] For example see (Dundes, 1988) for a wide-ranging discussion of Cinderella variants.

[4] Margaret Mills (1990) followed the transmission of stories through a circle of female tellers in Afghanistan. Mills documents how one story shifted between two tellers. Mills' study shows how change affects narrative pattern, genre, and meaning, demonstrating how shifts are conscious and creative processes on the teller's part.

[5] For a discussion of storytelling techniques in *Ramayana*, Stuart Blackburn's (1996) detailed study of a Tamil shadow puppet version,

describes the ways in which the puppeteers adapt, comment upon, and transform the narrative.

[6] The groundbreaking work on oral composition of Albert Lord (1960) has been developed by John Miles Foley (1988) and Ruth Finnegan (1992) among many others, exploring the delicate process of composition, improvisation, and use of oral formulas.

[7] See (Clayton 2004) for discussion on how images can be transmitted across linguistic boundaries.

[8] One of the tragedies of the tsunami was the destruction of these collections. Thankfully the craftsmen survived along with their knowledge of wood, mask dimension, and mythical characters.

[9] North Indian writer, Bharata Muni, wrote (sometime between 200 BC and 200 AD) on classical Sanskrit drama in *The Natyashastra* discussing in detail the various forms that rasa takes.

[10] Mr Chitrasena died in 2005, loved for his innovative interpretation of tradition.

[11] Kathak dancer, Amina Khayyam, worked with me in rehearsals to develop my use of gesture and movement.

[12] Ayhodha, Northern India.

[13] During 2005-2006 I worked with the British Library on *Inside Story*, a project with Yorkshire primary schools exploring *Ramayana*, among other epics. Children made their own monkeys, and the monkeys inspired the children to tell stories. The children's ideas then created a touring installation.

Bibliography

Stuart H. Blackburn, *Inside the Drama House: Rama Stories and Shadow Puppets in South India* (University of California Press, 1996).

William Buck, *Ramayana, King Rama's Way:Valmiki's* Ramayana *told in English prose* (University of California Press, 1976).

Flueckiger Burkhauter, Joyce and Laurie J. Sears, eds., *Boundaries of the Text: Epic Performances in South and Southeast Asia* (University of Michigan, 1991).

Sally Pomme Clayton, 'Telling the images' in *Estudos Literatura Oral Journal 9-10* (2004), pp.79-88.

Alan Dundes, ed., *Cinderella – A Casebook* (University of Wisconsin Press, 1988).

Ruth Finnegan, 'What is orality – if anything?' in *Byzantine Modern Greek Studies 14* (1990), pp.130-49.

R. Finnegan, *Oral Traditions and the Verbal Arts* (Routledge, 1992).

J.M. Foley, *The Theory of Oral Composition* (Bloomington Indiana, 1988).

Albert B. Lord, *The Singer of Tales* (Harvard University Press, 1960).

Margaret A. Mills, *Oral Narrative in Afghanistan: The Individual in Tradition* (Garland Publishing, 1990).

R.K. Narayan, *The Ramayana* (Vision Books, 1987).

Paula Richman, ed., *Many Ramayanas. The Diversity of a Narrative Tradition in South East Asia* (University of California Press, 1991).

Paula Richman, ed., *Questioning Ramayanas. A South Asian Tradition* (University of California Press, 2001).

5

Journalist as Storyteller:
Immersion Reporting

Sarah Niblock

Step into any offices of any newspaper and you will hear reporters and feature-writers swapping anecdotes about their latest 'tale' or 'yarn'. Storytelling is central to the craft of news journalism, especially in print, for it brings dry facts on a two-dimensional page to life, and beckons the reader to engage with the issues or events under scrutiny. While journalism stories tend not to conform to the standard narrative structure of beginning, middle and end – indeed the denouement has to be in the introductory paragraph [1] – they draw upon many of the characteristics of literary storytelling to transport the reader to the scene. Drama, conflict and raw human emotion are always at the forefront of journalism, whether the report is coming from a humanitarian crisis or from the council chamber at the local town hall. As journalists, we must describe unfolding events with such descriptive detail that the audience is transported to the very heart of the story in their mind's eye, so that they are compelled to read to the end. Journalism is all about competition, not only between rival news organisations but also on the page as each story competes with each other for your attention.

Journalism storytelling is also intertwined and frequently in conflict with the professional demands of a dynamic media industry. In the 21st century, the news production machine operates at an ever more frenetic pace. In the context of 24-hour rolling news and the increasing demand for online content in an instant, the priorities of reporting have shifted. Nowadays, following on from the reorganisations in newsrooms in the late 1980s and 1990s,[2] journalists are under pressure to keep the news short, simple, accessible and cheap. While the speed of new technology may have placed greater strictures upon some news journalists, for others, especially in the print sector, it has offered a way to break free. Newspapers and magazines are turning their attentions back to what they do best – in-depth narratives based on days, weeks, even months of meticulous first-hand reporting. In effect, print journalism is responding to readers who might get their first news snap from electronic media, but who ultimately still like to read.

Known as 'immersion reporting', a term coined in the US, this type of journalism is about taking the time to thoroughly unpack the subject under scrutiny, to enable a closer engagement on the part of the journalist so as to provide a full and unflinching analysis for the reader. Immersion journalism requires the writer to, as the name suggests, immerse ourselves in events or with the people we are reporting on. In this way, it is argued that the journalist is able to provide a more detailed, rounded and fully-nuanced report, which captures the context as well as the facts. Journalism is a human, subjective process, say immersion practitioners, so why try to adopt an objective façade when that is impossible to achieve? Instead, the journalist becomes an agent within the narrative, reflexively subverting the consensual notion of a reporter remaining an invisible eye-witness.

Recent prominent examples of immersion reporting might include the descriptive and emotive eye-witness narrative accounts of conflict, such as the journalism of the *Independent's* correspondent Robert Fisk. Music journalism, specifically profile interviews for *Rolling Stone* magazine, has tended to celebrate long periods of reporting activity on-the-road with the artist in question. More often, the quantity of detail gathered requires publication in book form. George Orwell's autobiographical *Down and Out in Paris and London* (1933) was an experiential account of life among the under-classes. Similarly, the celebrated work of 'gonzo' journalists Tom Wolfe and Hunter S. Thompson challenged the perceived boundaries between journalism and literature. More recently, Polly Toynbee's participant observation of experiences on the minimum wage have brought into sharper focus the means by which ordinary people live their lives in a constantly changing world. As 'reality' TV documents daily mundanity upon our screens, and as mainstream journalism sets out to portray reality as a single truth, immersionists seek to convey multiple viewpoints and a multiplicity of truths.

In his study of the resurgence of literary journalism Chris Harvey encapsulates how journalism is pressured into storytelling by other media: "Television. Hollywood movies. Even the computer game is interactive storytelling. It has a protagonist and challengers and story structure and rising action and ... a denouement". [3] With the pressing commercial imperatives of journalism, especially alongside the proliferation in new media, newspapers and magazines are searching for new ways to engage with their readers. News audiences are declining. In the United States, three recent studies – by the Project for Excellence in Journalism in 2004, the Pew Research Centre in 2005, and The Media Centre (at the American Press Institute) in 2005 – signal a "long-term decline in news consumption". [4] A survey among American 18 to 34-year-olds carried out in May 2004 shows that, with the exception of Web portals, the vast majority of them rarely, if ever, turn to the news in any medium. [5]

My own background centres on print news where, in the past 20 years, I have seen a loosening of the conventional ties that force the writer to be an invisible mediator. News journalism has traditionally been characterised as a 'top down' approach. Earlier in my own career, sitting in editorial meetings, senior staff would select stories based on their notions of what was important, choosing sources and packaging the story as they deemed appropriate. [6] Now news consumers are too distrustful of the integrity and perceived narrow scope of the journalistic media. [7] More than ever, it is our readers and their lives and interests that help shape the news agenda, and they want that to be reflected through a more human approach to the news.

Simultaneously, there has been a renewed interest in reflexive forms of journalism, which make the journalist part of the story and which make transparent the processes of news gathering and reporting. As a journalist, I have found that the gap between the reporter and the report*ed* has closed. When I first trained as a journalist, I was taught that my presence within a story was purely as a mediator, not as an agent. Yet soon, on my local newspaper, I was charting my experiences week-by-week as I learnt to drive, donated blood and even how I felt as I watched the Princess of Wales comfort families made homeless by flooding in north Wales. I was becoming part of the news, an average young woman with whom readers could identify and, hopefully, share the experience more acutely through my words.

This approach has become evident even in the mainstream, especially in conflict reporting post 9/11. The expanded first-person accounts of veteran foreign affairs correspondents such as the aforementioned Fisk and John Simpson (BBC) and Lindsey Hilsum (Channel 4 News) follow in the steps of Hemingway and Martha Gellhorn, who used first-person narratives and detailed descriptions. Significantly, the reliance on local stringers in war-zones hard to access by Western journalists has brought a wider array of sources and viewpoints into the news media. [8]

It is unsurprising that this form of journalism has been resurgent and popularised in the US and is now taught as a module at some J-schools. America has the tradition of literary journalism referred to as New Journalism, which embraced a narrative drive. The term New Journalism was originated by Matthew Arnold in 1887 as he described W.T. Stead's writing in the *Pall Mall Gazette*. What distinguished New Journalism practitioners in the 1960s and early 1970s was not that they were doing something different but that so many were doing it simultaneously. Tom Wolfe, one of the pioneers, impelled journalists and writers alike to subvert literary boundaries. Wolfe, who was writing for the New York *Herald Tribune*, wanted to be more than 'just' a reporter, with all the job's associations of dispassionate style and concise structure. His dream, like that of so many journalists, was to become a novelist. But while scratching a living as a reporter, he saw no reason why his twin talents might not merge in order to produce lengthy writerly features.

In his book, *The New Journalism* (1973), Wolfe rejected the notion that the reporter's tone should be impersonal or that any sense of the writer's presence be underplayed so as not to turn off readers: "When they came across that pale beige tome, it began to signal them, unconsciously, that a known bore was here again, 'the journalist', a pedestrian mind, a phlegmatic spirit, a faded personality, and there was no way to get rid of the pallid little troll, short of ceasing to read."[9]

Whereas the convention of journalism has traditionally been to inform the audience, allowing them to form their own judgements based on facts, Wolfe and his contemporaries, such as Hunter S. Thompson and Truman Capote, sought to present a richer and more detailed, descriptive array of facts. To do otherwise, it was argued, would be to present the reader with an incomplete picture. Wolfe's contemporary, the journalist and author Dan Wakefield, writing in *The Atlantic Monthly*, defined the style as "imaginative" reporting that enhances the uptake of facts: "[the journalist] has presented them in a full instead of a naked manner, brought out the sights, sounds and feel surrounding those facts, and connected them by comparison with other facts of history, society, and literature in an artistic manner that does not diminish but gives great depth and dimension to the facts."[10]

While it might appear that the focus is on literary style, this form of journalism came into its own as a methodical system of data collection. One of the main formats for information gathering by a journalist is the interview, face-to-face or more frequently in high-pressure time-poor contexts, by telephone. The method favoured by immersion reporters is shadowing, whereby they observe unobtrusively the detailed verbal and non-verbal behaviour of their subjects. Wolfe maintained that this method ensured a more effective determination of the subjects' genuine character as opposed to a façade adopted for the given moment of the interview. His 1968 book *The Electric Kool-Aid Acid Test* immerses Wolfe within the psychedelic world of Ken Kesey and the Merry Pranksters and their bus journey across America. The text is synonymous with 1960s counter-culture, charting encounters with the Hell's Angels, their take-over of a church convention and cat and mouse chase with the law. In his author's notes, Wolfe describes the immersionism and 360-degree view of the journey: "All the events, details and dialogue I have recorded are either what I saw and heard myself or were told to me by people who were there themselves or were recorded on tapes or film or in writing ... The Pranksters recorded much of their own history in the Prankster Archives in the form of tapes, diaries, letters, photographs and the 40-hour movie of the bus trip."

Current practitioners do not call it New Journalism anymore, preferring terms like 'creative non-fiction' or even 'fly-on-the wall journalism', characterised by the broadcast and print work of Louis Theroux and Nick Broomfield. But they still share the emphasis on dialogue, detail and slice-of-life details. Periodicals such as *Rolling Stone*, *Village Voice* and the style magazine *Vice* have offered a home for younger more experimental journalists searching for a space for more creative expression and interpretation of news and current affairs. *Vice*'s issue V3N11 was tag-lined the "immersionism issue". It published a series of illustrated features, titles beginning with 'Living With', including refugees, terrorists, drunks and prostitutes and even infamous rock star Pete Doherty. [11]

James E. Murphy has identified three specific characteristics of immersion journalism. Firstly, there is the use of adverbs, adjectives and dialogue to transport the reader to the scene. Secondly, the reporter recognises and imparts their subjectivity as opposed to impartial detachment. They interpret events as they see them rather than trying to write as if they were but a faceless conduit. Thirdly, there is immersion, the act of being absorbed experientially in the story. [12] The journalist will spend a great deal of time in the situation or with the person they are reporting on. Immersion reporting must be anchored in factual information. Their dialogue and scenarios must be about events and conversations they have participated in directly or else have witnessed. Kramer (1995) identifies how dialogue and fact is interspersed with contextual digressions that serve to provide context. [13]

George Orwell's *Down and Out in Paris and London*, first published in 1933 is his personal autobiographical account of living in poverty in both cities. It begins in Paris, where Orwell lived for two years, attempting to survive by giving English lessons and contributing reviews and articles to various periodicals. He ended up working as a *plongeur*, the most menial kitchen helper, where he earned barely sufficient money to feed himself. Orwell used scene-by-scene construction, vignettes of reality, as the building block of his reportage, distinguishing it from traditional journalism. Each short chapter recounts an experience. Whereas a conventional journalist will 'tell' the reader about a place or person, Orwell 'showed' them to his reader. Here he highlights the contrasting scenes in the dining room and behind the kitchen door, as he describes how a head waiter serves food after giving an apprentice a dressing down:

> 'Tu me fais chier. Do you call yourself a waiter, you young bastard? You a waiter! You're not fit to scrub floors in the brothel your mother came from. Maquereau!'
> Words failing him, he turned to the door; and as he opened it he farted loudly, a favourite Italian insult.
> Then he entered the dining room and sailed across it dish in hand, as graceful as a swan. [14]

Orwell concludes the vignette by commenting on how the customer must have felt like they were being served by an aristocrat, in such a manner that any sense of detachment between the writer and reader disappears. We see the scene and interpret it through Orwell's field of vision.

A parallel with mainstream journalism is that all scenes must contain action. In news journalism, editors demand that something is happening. Journalism, in all its guises, has to be active; even when something is not happening there is activity because we are anticipating something. *The Guardian* journalist Polly Toynbee's first-hand account of living on the breadline, *Hard Work: Life in Low Pay Britain* (2003) describes in minute and vivid detail the effort that goes into sustaining a basic everyday existence in poverty. She describes the breakneck pace of her life and mind in minutiae as she negotiates telesales, cake factories and hospital work whilst living on a disadvantaged council estate. In doing so, she illuminates the sheer effort and drain behind ordinary lives that to mainstream journalism appear uneventful. She spares no detail in describing how she puts up a curtain in her flat, as if the whole event has consumed every last bit of her mental and physical energy:

> … bought ten long nails for 20p and hammered them across the top of the windows with my shoe. The plaster crumbled a bit and the heels of my shoes took a lot of damage but the nails held, so I tied up the bootlaces across them … looking up at other people's windows, I noticed several had strange make-shift arrangements much like mine, presumably for the same reason. Curtain rails are expensive and hard to fix. [15]

Whereas Toynbee's immersion charts the everyday, slice-of-life that is all too familiar yet untold, the Polish author and journalist Ryszard Kapuscinski journeys into unfamiliar territory. He is best known in the English-speaking world for his reporting from Africa in the 1960s and 1970s, when he witnessed first-hand the continent's liberation from colonialism. Starting in the early 1960s, Kapuscinski has published books of increasing literary craftsmanship characterized by sophisticated narrative techniques and psychological portraits. He employs an array of stylization and uncanny metaphors to interpret the world as he sees it. His background knowledge allows him to synthesise localised issues into wider global problems, as he told *The Journal of the International Institute*:

> My writing is a combination of three elements. The first is travel: not travel like a tourist, but travel as exploration, as concentration, as a purpose. The second is reading literature on the subject: books, articles, scholarship. The third is reflection, which comes from travel and reading. My books are created from a combination of these three elements. [16]

His detailed description operates as a symbolic 'reading' of the hidden sense of the scenes he encounters, confronting the reader with feelings of engagement and identification. This extract describes the smell of the tropics: "We instantly recognise its weight, its sticky materiality. The smell makes us at once aware that we are at that point on earth where an exuberant and indefatigable nature labours, incessantly reproducing itself, spreading and blooming, even as it sickens, disintegrates, festers and decays." [17]

Kapuscinski also ushers the reader towards identifications with key players, in this case with himself as a child in 1939, though also by extension with any child caught up in conflict:

> I see gigantic fountains of earth spraying up into the air. I want to run towards this extraordinary spectacle which stuns and fascinates me, because, having as yet no wartime experiences, I am unable to connect into a single chain of cause and effect those shining silver planes, the thunder of the bombs, the plumes of earth flying up to the height of the trees, and the danger of imminent death. [18]

While the 1980s may have ushered in an emphasis on fast, frenetic news on the run, the 21st century is being marked by a renewed emphasis on longer expositions. In an ideal world, you get both. War reporting has been a common area of literary journalism, including John Steinbeck's reports of the Second World War, Martha Gellhorn on the Spanish Civil War and Michael Herr's hallucinatory depictions of Vietnam. If we look at the contemporary work of conflict reporter Robert Fisk, we see that, compared with the traditional inverted pyramid, [19] the narrative style is better at conveying the non-linear chaos of war. It can better convey the multiplicity of 'truths' present in any conflict. And it can more honestly communicate the horrors of ceaseless bombardment and ensuing suffering, which cannot be neatly accounted for in a 25-word introduction. [20] Fisk's one-week diary of life in Beirut in the early days of the 2006 Lebanon/Israel conflict provides an atmosphere and intimacy with the afflicted that would be hard to communicate in any other way. Here Fisk describes a close encounter with a missile:

Sunday 16 July

… this morning, Abed and I actually see one pierce the smoke above us. 'Habibi,' (my friend!) he cries, and I start screaming 'Turn the car around, turn it round' and we drive away for our lives from the southern suburbs. As we turn the corner there is a shattering explosion and mountain of grey smoke blossoming from the road we have just left. [21]

Fisk's writing is characterised by a reflexivity that illuminates the construction of mainstream news reports. On 21st July 2006 he described critically how camera crews and journalists filmed some of the first evacuations from Beirut:

Even the newspapers and magazines managed to avoid the reality. As our Jolly Tars helped the elderly on board and US Marines landed very briefly – or 'stormed the beach', to quote the Associated Press's imperishable report – to protect their ship, television crews hunted through the crowds of refugees for suitable pictures … inexorably towards the very few blue-eyed men and blonde ladies of the 'kith and kin' variety … It was pathetic. [22]

But in this sense might not the role of the news journalist as a storyteller be in conflict with that of an impartial mediator? The renewed interest in narrative is resurrecting long-held concerns about sourcing and accuracy. Criticism of New Journalism style continued more than a decade on when in 1981, *Washington Post* reporter Janet Cooke was stripped of a Pulitzer Prize after it was discovered she has fabricated the eight-year-old heroin addict in her feature lead. *Los Angeles Times* media critic David Shaw commented in the *American Journalism Review* in December 1981 [23] that Cooke had fallen into a trap: "Janet Cooke wrote very well. Too well. She forgot she was a journalist, not a storyteller – a reporter, not a creator." Similarly, Bob Woodward, famed for his role in exposing the Watergate affair, has had to defend the integrity of his sourcing in his book *Veil: The Secret Wars of the CIA*. [24] One of the underlying fears on the part of journalists who criticise narrative approaches is that a book is a very different outlet from a newspaper or magazine. While book-length journalism is, in effect, a product of the author, newspapers and magazines are team efforts and institutions with reputations which could be rocked by any accusation of mis-reporting or editorialisation. Lengthy, elaborate and descriptive sentences can bring a location or person vividly into the mind's eye, but does the reader become distracted by it so they do not recognise or assess the writer's overriding viewpoint?

There is the danger that immersion journalists might be seduced by their extraordinary access to their subjects. This criticism has been levelled against, amongst others, the writer Truman Capote who, following the success of his short story *Breakfast at Tiffany's* [25], produced a piece of book-length journalism about a family's murder. *In Cold Blood* [26] was researched and written over a period of five years, during which time Capote spent long periods of time in the company of one of the convicted murderers on death row, thanks to bungs to the prison chief. It is alleged that Capote's fascination with Perry Smith grew overly intimate, yet simultaneously exploitative. In employing a lawyer to try to get Smith and his accomplice Richard Hickock a reprieve, it has been alleged that Capote was buying time to persuade the killers to describe in their own eyes what happened on the night of the murder to boost the book. [27]

I confess that on the two occasions that I was asked to do

something akin to immersion reporting, I refused. The first request, in the early 1990s, involved me going into a Liverpool nightclub to see how quickly I could buy the rave drug Ecstasy, then writing about my experience, with covert images, the following day. I was encouraged by my editor, who said: "You will get an award for this." I declined because as a local journalist, you are often recognisable within your community and, at that point, I would have been putting my own life and that of those closest to me in danger at a time when police were already working undercover to extract evidence anyway. The interest to the public outweighed public interest, and that view was subsequently supported by my editor. The second time I refused was when a best-selling UK women's glossy magazine asked me and a male partner to take a series of lessons from a tantric sex instructor and share our experiences in detail. I am no prude and had written about sex for that magazine and others before. But there is something in the news reporter training that may actually attract those who would rather hide behind the machinery of print journalism than be on the page.

Despite the caveats, immersion journalism is on the ascent. This chapter has focused upon print incarnations, while it is a form that fits very well with the internet. The use of multiple perspectives can be presented through links, which take the viewer to different sites. [28] In *Deciding What's News* (1979), Herbert Gans proposed a two-tier model of multi-perspective journalism. According to this model, there should be a centralized tier of mainstream linear journalism across several media forms and secondly a decentralised series of alternative news forms offering more specialised or niche views. [29] This chapter has hopefully shown that the forms of journalistic storytelling are shifting and dynamic and, just as Wolfe and others have smudged the once-demarcated boundaries between journalism and literature, so may the demands of audiences who have seen the potential new media formats. As the authority and adequacy of the journalist and eyewitness continues to be undermined, so we may see a further shift towards alternative 'truth-tellers' who have lived the story. This has been witnessed recently in the work of stand up comedians such as Mark Thomas, who has interrogated US and UK complicity in the arms and torture trade. Russell Brand early in his MTV career, lived on camera alongside those on the margins of society such as prostitutes and racists, and now reflexively charts his former life as a drug-user to large audiences and through journalism.

Dry information, however intrinsically significant, cannot be presented as a list of facts. It must undergo a human process of packaging and presentation to attract the reader. News-writing, at its best, is weaving a narrative that connects an array of facts, views and descriptions, garnered from a range of sources. It should resonate and stimulate as well as inform. In this way good writing and good reporting reinforce one another and serve the purpose of informing and engaging the public.

Notes
[1] Sarah Niblock, *Inside Journalism* (Blueprint, 1996), p.29.
[2] Iain Stevenson, 'Profits and The Public Interest: The Business of Newspapers' in Richard Keeble, ed., *Print Journalism: A Critical Introduction*, (Routledge, 2006), pp.40-1.
[3] Chris Harvey, 'Tom Wolfe's Revenge: The Renewed Interest in Literary Journalism' in *American Journalism Review* (October 1994), p.41.
[4] Pew Research Centre (2005). *Trends 2005*, p.44, http://pewresearch.org/trends.
[5] Merrill Brown, 'Abandoning the news', *Carnegie Reporter* 3(2), Spring 2005. http://www.carnegie.org/reporter/10/news/index.html.
[6] See David Machin and Sarah Niblock, *News Production: Theory and Practice* (Routledge, 2006).
[7] According to a 10-country opinion poll for the BBC, Reuters, and The Media Centre, published on 3rd May 2006, UK citizens are strikingly similar to those in the US regarding many of their attitudes to the media. Like those in the US, they are much less likely than citizens in other parts of the world to think that the media reports all sides of a story, with 64 per cent disagreeing that the media achieves this. Also 43 per cent disagree that the media reports news accurately. http://www.globescan.com/news_archives/bbcreut.html.
[8] David Machin and Sarah Niblock (2006), ibid.
[9] Tom Wolfe, *The New Journalism* (HarperCollins, 1973), p.17.
[10] David Wakefield, 'The Personal Voice and the Impersonal Eye' in *The Atlantic Monthly*, June 1966, pp.86-90.
[11] http://www.viceland.com/issues_uk/v3n11/htdocs/index.php
[12] James E. Murphy, 'The New Journalism: A Critical Perspective', paper presented to the Association for Education in Journalism, San Diego, 1974.

[13] Mark Kramer, 'Breakable Rules for Literary Journalists' in Norman Sims and Mark Kramer, eds., *Literary Journalism: A New Collection of the Best American Nonfiction* (Ballantine Books, 1995).

[14] George Orwell, *Down and Out in Paris and London* (Penguin, 1940), pp.67-8.

[15] Polly Toynbee, *Hard Work: Life in Low Pay Britain* (Bloomsbury, London, 2003), p.49.

[16] http://www.umich.edu/~iinet/journal/vol6no1/kapuschinski.html

[17] Ryszard Kapuscinski, *The Shadow of the Sun* (Vintage, 2002), p.4.

[18] Ryszard Kapuscinski, 'When There is Talk of 1945' in *Granta* 88, 15 December 2004, http://www.granta.com/extracts/2226

[19] H. Pottker, 'News and its Communicative Quality: The Inverted Pyramid – When and Why did it Appear?' in *Journalism Studies*, Vol. 4, No. 4, November 2003, pp.501-11.

[20] Richard Keeble, *Print Journalism: A Critical Introduction* (Routledge, 2006), p.333.

[21] Robert Fisk, 'War: Lebanon: Special Report: A gripping diary of one week in the life and death of Beirut' in the *Independent on Sunday*, 23rd July 2006, p.39.

[22] Robert Fisk, 'This is not Dunkirk. This is Munich' in the *Independent*, 21st July 2006, p.10.

[23] *American Journalism Review* (December 1981).

[24] Bob Woodward, *Veil: The Secret Wars of the CIA* (Simon and Schuster, 2005).

[25] Truman Capote, *Breakfast at Tiffany's* (Penguin, 2000).

[26] Truman Capote, *In Cold Blood* (Penguin, 2000).

[27] See Gerald Clarke, *Capote: A Biography* (Simon and Schuster, 1988), pp. 356-7.

[28] See salon.com and slate.com for examples.

[29] Herbert Gans, *Deciding What's News* (Pantheon Books, 1979), pp.317-18.

6

Storyworld:
Or, How I Learned How to Write a Novel

David Rain

A story is a world. Let's call it Storyworld.

As a child I wrote easily, fluently. Story after story flowed from me – pirate adventures, mysteries, science fiction extravaganzas, all of them no doubt awful, and plundered shamelessly from things I had read or seen on television. This didn't matter: Storyworld was open to me. I never had to look for the key.

Many of us recall such childhood fluency. It's a wonderful gift, and usually it's deceptive. It gives us the idea that writing is easy. For a few, it remains so: Enid Blyton, notoriously, could turn out a Famous Five novel in a week. [1] But for most of us, writing becomes not only harder, but *immensely* harder as we grow older. When I became an adult, my writing stalled – and stayed stalled for years. The problem wasn't coming up with characters or plots or constructing scenes: I've always found that easy. What I couldn't do was place these things convincingly in a particular world.

Many writers, I'm certain, don't give this a moment's thought. They write their story, and it's set in Lagos or Los Angeles or the East End of London because this is the world they know, and that's all there is to it. I never felt I had a natural world to write about.

Although I presently live in England, I grew up in a small town in Australia with an intensely English mother who reminisced continually about life back home – even now, her memories of London in the Blitz seem to me more real than some of my own experiences. Australia to me was an alien land where I didn't belong. So far as I was concerned, I was English – although I should add that England, where I had never been, was to me a country consisting largely of castles, boarding schools and country houses in which weekend guests were likely to be murdered in bizarre circumstances, requiring the intervention of a brilliant amateur detective.

Needless to say, the real England has been something of a disappointment.

The problem for me as a writer was this: I couldn't *do* England and I couldn't *do* Australia – or rather, I couldn't in either case render in fiction the recognisable, contemporary reality which I assumed to be the be-all and end-all of 'serious' writing. My imagination kept slipping off elsewhere. What I had, though it took me a long time to realise it, was the classic profile of a science fiction, fantasy, or historical novelist.

Anyone who wants to write fiction should answer this question: 'Why do we read it?' I'd say that reading fiction, when it goes well, is an experience of immersion in a writer's world. Where creating worlds is concerned, the imaginary mythological lands depicted by J.R.R. Tolkien in *The Hobbit* (1937) and *The Lord of the Rings* (1954-5) may be taken as an extreme example. [2] And yet there is a sense in which all writers are Tolkien. Whether a writer draws directly from life, or invents outrageously, is neither here nor there. The task is always the same: to build Storyworld.

Here's how I made a Storyworld of my own.

*　　*　　*

The first stirrings of my fantasy series *The Orokon*, published under my pseudonym Tom Arden, [3] came in an unfinished story I began in 1989 called 'The Astronomer's House'. I don't remember much about it, except that it concerned a boy on the run in what appeared to be the 18th century. On the top of the manuscript I wrote: *This is it*. But *it* sat on the page and didn't go anywhere.

Some years later, I visited the Czech Republic for the first time. In those days, not long after the Velvet Revolution, the country appeared much less western than it does today: no advertising billboards, no McDonald's, few cars on the roads. All this filled me with a curious fascination. One night, on a train somewhere in the Bohemian countryside, I looked out at the darkness and had the sensation of finding myself in an alternative reality: one like ours but strange, different in innumerable ways. At once I knew I wanted to write a book set in an imaginary world, with its own countries, governments, armies, wars, intrigues, and bizarre magical happenings.

Of course I realised I wasn't the first person to think of this. I began to research the epic fantasy. The form was fascinating. Perhaps the only genre to span the divide between 'young adult' and 'adult' fiction,[4] the fantasy novel, of the kind influenced by Tolkien, is an endlessly ramifying, extravagant romance, in the true literary meaning of the word – an exotic otherworldly adventure story with a huge cast of characters, endless subplots and twisting labyrinths of story, all of it held together by the most classic of structures: the quest.[5]

I'll admit I was more impressed by the *idea* of such books than by many of the actual epic fantasies I read. This didn't bother me. I'd write the sort of epic fantasy I wanted to read – funny, frightening, satirical, scurrilous, and *not* filled with cardboard macho heroes having swordfights.

The problem was how to start. Usually, if you're writing a novel, you begin with a character or situation. In epic fantasy, you'd be advised to start with the world: it determines so much else.

Most epic fantasies, following Tolkien, draw on the Middle Ages, no doubt because of its possibilities for chainmail, broadswords, axes, and hot oil poured from battlements. I based the *Orokon* world on 18th-century Europe, not so much to be original but because I knew more about it than any other period, having studied 18th-century literature and later taught courses about it at university level. Besides, it would be glamorous: powdered wigs, ball gowns, duelling pistols, contending armies in red and blue.

The first thing I did was to invent imaginary countries: England-like Ejland and its oppressed colony of Zenzau; the *Arabian Nights* kingdom of Unang Lia; the half-Greek, half-Caribbean island realms of Wenaya. I drew maps.

Side by side with geography came the religion of the *Orokon*-world, a whole pantheon of gods: the irascible Ur-God Orok and his five variously petulant or boorish children – Koros, Viana, Theron, Javander, and Agonis, each of whom would be the god of a particular nation. Numerous sub-deities, devils, and monsters soon followed, notably the anti-god Toth-Vexrah, the ultimate villain of the series.

Science fiction and fantasy writers call this kind of thing 'world-building'. It's like piecing together a puzzle. First of all, work out what you'll need – then fill in the gaps. Contrasts provide a clue: if one country is like *this*, another will be like *that*. If there's a god of light, there'll be a god of darkness. All these things become engines of story. Contrast two characters, two countries: either way, you're setting up conflict.

World-building becomes daunting in several ways.

For one thing, there's the sheer amount of *stuff* you need to fill out an invented world. Take, for example, time. Are there 24 hours in a day? Is there a week, lasting seven days? Is there a day called Thursday? All these things have to be thought about, and you have to know the answers. [6]

There are all the real-world things that can't be mentioned. Music and acting play a huge part in *The Orokon*, but the composers and operas, plays and playwrights all have to be invented: I can't just say "Shakespeare" and be done with it. (The possibilities for parody, however, are immense.)

It's important to stress that everything can't be made up. Details generally draw on real-world parallels. A story in which *every* element – customs, manners, art, religion, politics, environment – was wholly bizarre and alien would soon become tiresome. It would also sink under the weight of explanation.

How much do you need to know when you start? The trick is to invent only as much as you need to get the story under way. If you're not going to get to Wenaya until Book Four (and I didn't), how much do you need to know about it now? Maybe not so much as you think, other than that it's there.

A major problem is how to keep world-building in its place. All this information has to be worked into the story naturally. It can't be thrown at the reader in huge gobbets – what science fiction readers call, evocatively enough, 'info-dumping'. The background is precisely that – a background. The foreground is the story.

The first *Orokon* book, *The Harlequin's Dance*, begins – as do many epic fantasies – with a mythological prologue. Its purpose is to show the reader strange gods and legends, portending the otherwordly happenings to follow.

The main story then starts simply. The first chapters show the meeting, on the day of a village fair, between a crippled boy called Jem and a half-feral girl called Cata. These will be the hero and the heroine of the story. Cata lives with her father, a blind hermit, in a cave in the woods, while Jem, for his part, is entirely helpless, pushed about in a bath chair by his fat and fussy Aunt Umbecca, a puritanical religious fanatic for whom Cata conceives an immediate dislike.

Jem longs for a freedom it seems he will never know. His uncle Tor, a notorious rebel in Ejland's recent civil war, inspires him with useless dreams. But things change when Jem meets a mysterious dwarf, Barnabas, who coaxes him out of the bath chair and teaches him to walk on crutches. Encouraged by the dwarf, Jem begins to think that one day he'll really walk. It seems he will.

Unfortunately, Jem's Aunt Umbecca is deep in the thrall of the slimy local physician, Goodman Waxwell, her partner in religious fanaticism. Goodman Waxwell is by no means impressed that Jem can walk on crutches. Is this not to defy the will of the Lord Agonis? To Goodman Waxwell, physical deformities are undoubtedly evidence of divine displeasure, a source of moral and spiritual pollution. Might it not be advisable to amputate the little lad's legs?

It's not exactly a gentle story. But it's tight, particular, and focused on character. As it advances, the story opens out massively; by the time it's through, there will have been magic and marvels in abundance. But magic and marvels are seldom interesting in themselves, or rather they aren't for more than five minutes. It's people that drive a story. Give us people – interesting, living people – and we'll follow them, possibly to the strangest places. Forget the people, and the book will be dull, no matter how brilliant the world-building.

A story is people. Always. [7]

*   *   *

It's also structure.

If I had one problem with *The Orokon* right away, it was how to structure something so long and complex as an epic fantasy. I knew

I needed a quest: an epic fantasy has a quest as a murder mystery has a murder. Quests, among their many advantages, provide overarching dramatic focus in long and complex novels, something clear and simple that can be explained in a sentence.

But a quest for what? And why?

Following the example of the early David Eddings, I'd decided that *The Orokon* should run for five volumes. But volume-divisions in the Eddings series are somewhat arbitrary. [8] I realised that *The Orokon* would have greater shape and unity if some magical token or talisman were searched for and found in each book – the whole series, in other words, would recount a quest, but in each book there would also be a sub-quest, on the way to the greater goal.

A good piece of advice for a writer is to steal wherever you can – barring outright plagiarism – and the structure I decided on was plundered from the BBC-TV science fiction series, *Doctor Who*. In the season *The Key to Time*, first screened in 1978-9, a cosmic overlord called the White Guardian sends the Doctor on a mission to find the scattered segments of the cube-shaped 'key', which have to be reassembled, pieced together like a puzzle, in order to restore the harmony of the universe. Unfortunately there's also a Black Guardian, and he has other ideas.

The Key to Time consists of six serial stories, each of which can be understood on its own, and each of which ends with one segment of the key being found. [9]

This gave me my quest. In *The Orokon* there are five missing crystals, each of which embodies the powers of one of the five children of the Ur-God Orok. There are five books; therefore one crystal is found, by Jem and his companions, in each book. The purpose of finding them is to save the universe from destruction by the anti-god, Toth-Vexrah, whose time has at last come – and naturally he's keen on grabbing the crystals for himself.

Structure, of course, is only a container. By itself, it doesn't make a book good or bad. *The Orokon* works, if it does, because of the vivid and varied characters, the grotesque black comedy, the bizarre adventures, the wild magic. But structure is what keeps it all together: the goblet that holds the wine.

Other elements fell rapidly into place.

It was clear to me from the first that the series needed a love story running all through it. Where there was Jem, there was soon Cata. I knew the story would be more interesting if Cata was contrasted greatly with Jem in background, abilities and character. But if Jem and Cata fell in love in the first book, they couldn't be allowed to go through four further books in loving bliss all the way. They would have to be divided, in the most dramatic way possible, by the end of the first book, and kept apart for long periods after that. They would come back together in the third book, only to be parted again.

The *Orokon* world, as I've suggested, is the 18th century seen through a distorting mirror. But five volumes is a long haul. Backgrounds had to be varied from book to book, as the quest moved from country to country within the invented world. In addition, each book had to have independent story arcs that could be resolved within that book, while keeping the greater quest in view, escalating the stakes, and propelling readers towards the next episode.

Structure is a wonderful thing. Two things happened once I'd worked out the rationale of the series. First of all, I sold it – all five volumes – on the basis of 50 pages and an outline. Second, I found that within the structure I was free to do much as I liked, so long as the quest was always kept in view.

As the series proceeded, I found I was undermining as much as indulging the conventions of epic fantasy. Books like this are expected to follow a formula, ending with the young hero installed at last in his rightful place on the throne. Let's just say that *The Orokon* doesn't end like that. A number of readers have been disappointed, even enraged at the ending. I'm unrepentant.

Then comes the question of style.

I remember being impressed by a remark a friend once made that 18th-century novels seemed more 'experimental' than 19th-century novels, because narrative conventions at that time had not yet hardened and set. Since I was writing, in effect, an 18th-century novel, I used the full range of 18th-century techniques: interpolated tales (stories inset within the larger story); sections set out in letter form; blatant addresses to the reader from the author. To keep the texture interesting, I also wrote parts of the narrative as dramatic scripts, with dialogue and stage directions, and in the fourth volume an important part of the plot is revealed through the performance of a classical play, written in blank verse.

The Orokon, with all its varieties of style and proliferations of plot, became, in effect, a massive folding-in of all my past reading, all my old obsessions: Dickens, Shakespeare, Doctor Who, Dan Dare, Robin Hood and Robinson Crusoe, pirate movies, William Blake, DC and Marvel Comics, Kate Bush (inspiration for Cata), Stanley Kubrick's movie of *Barry Lyndon*, which taught me how to do 18th-century battle scenes – they're all in there. It's rather as if I had a magic box and stuffed into it everything from my childhood and my youth, before it was too late.

* * *

The Orokon taught me how to write a novel.

Some of the things I learned are, in a sense, negative: things I'd do differently another time. I shan't expand: authors shouldn't criticise their own work in public. There are enough people out there only too keen to do that for us. But here are two lessons I've learned.

One is that creativity isn't a continuous state of rapture. Earlier, as I struggled to write novels, I'd always been looking for the great idea, the *This is it* moment, and been disappointed when one idea after another turned to dust. But dust is inevitable in the building trade. I wasn't prepared for how boring writing can be, how dull and plodding, in the early stages. Many a project was abandoned because I looked at it and said, "This is dead on the page." In truth, I hadn't given it a chance to live.

During the years of working on *The Orokon*, I became so immersed in it that it felt intensely real to me. But that immersion didn't happen all at once. The inspiration – that night in the Czech Republic – was brief, a fleeting moment. The research, the map-making and the structural plans were all, for the most part, sheer dogged work, a laying of foundations. Everything I've written starts like this. Inspiration – that nervous anticipation, that sudden soaring thrill – comes back, but only when the work is well advanced. Writing is love. But you have to prove yourself worthy.

A second lesson I learned was about self-expression.

For years I'd fretted over how to 'express myself' in fiction, as if my aim in writing was to impose on the world my character or personality. (Egotism like this is typical of young male writers.) What

I didn't realise was that writing has a way of curving back on itself, bringing you back to where you are. I'd thought I had to write about my life realistically; instead, by writing fantasy, I found I'd expressed all my real concerns anyway. Magic crystals were never the point. The quest was my own quest to discover myself. The crippled boy who learns to walk was, in a sense, me; but I was all the other characters in *The Orokon* too – gods, goddesses, kings and queens, commoners, heroes and villains, every one of them was an aspect of myself.

A novelist's concern should be telling a story: self-expression happens while you're looking the other way.

The Orokon is a million words long and took seven years to write. For four of those years, I worked on the books full-time, doing little else except getting up at six o'clock every morning and writing for twelve hours, day after day. By the time the last book was finished, I was left battered and depleted.

Often I wondered if it had all been worth it. I hadn't become rich and famous. I'd thrown in my job teaching English. I wasn't at all sure what to do next. I slipped into a vague but debilitating malaise. For a time I turned my back on *The Orokon*. I didn't want to think about it and didn't want to talk about it. To have spent so much of my life writing *fantasy* seemed, indeed, shaming. [10]

I tried writing in different styles, discovering new techniques. Some things worked and some didn't. I realised I could write stories set in the so-called real world: it's all Storyworld, once the story starts. Slowly I crept out from under the spell of *The Orokon*. But slowly, too, I came to see that I owed everything to this creaky old magic toybox. It had shown me the way into Storyworld.

I shan't be leaving anytime soon.

Notes

[1] Blyton at her peak published 15 to 20 children's books a year. "All it takes, really, is imagination," she told a journalist. See Barbara Stoney, *Enid Blyton: The Biography* (1974; rev. ed. Hodder and Stoughton, 1992), p.142.

[2] A term devised by Tolkien, "Secondary World" – as opposed to the "Primary World", or world in which we live – is often used to describe such invented realms. It's clear, however, from Tolkien's use of the term,

that he doesn't apply it only to outright fantasy: the Secondary World, what I call Storyworld, is where *all* stories unfold. See Tolkien, 'On Fairy-stories', in *Tree and Leaf* (Allen and Unwin, 1964), pp.11-70; esp. pp.36-7, 44-5. This essay has greatly influenced my thinking about fantasy and fiction generally.

[3] People often ask me why I don't publish fiction under my own name. Anyone who has written under another name knows the answer. Pseudonyms liberate us from the burden of personality and all its inhibitions – or seem to, which for writing purposes is the same thing. And names *do* matter. 'George Orwell' isn't the same person as 'Eric Blair', his real name. 'Mark Twain' isn't the same as 'Samuel Langhorne Clemens'.

[4] Fan-mail suggests that the typical *Orokon* reader is in the late teens – although many are well into adulthood. Male and female seem divided roughly equally.

[5] Popular modern fantasy epics include Terry Brooks' *The Sword of Shannara* (1977) and its sequels; Stephen Donaldson's six-volume *Chronicles of Thomas Covenant the Unbeliever* (1977-83); David Eddings' linked quintets *The Belgariad* (1982-4) and *The Malloreon* (1987-91); and Robert Jordan's 'Wheel of Time' sequence, which began with *The Eye of the World* (1990).

[6] Thursday is 'Thor's Day', from Norse mythology. Wednesday is 'Woden's Day'. But what if you're writing about a world where the Norse gods were unknown? We might add that the month of August is named after the Emperor Augustus. For my solution to the time problem, see 'Appendix: Time in *The Orokon*', in the first volume, *The Harlequin's Dance*.

[7] Of course 'ideas' have a significance in science fiction and fantasy that they often don't have in so-called 'general fiction': for example, H.G. Wells' *The Time Machine* (1895) initially impresses us simply with the *idea* of such an invention. But the idea is carried by the story of a human adventurer. Olaf Stapledon's *Last and First Men* (1930), a sort of history-book of the future, is a rare example of a work devoted solely to world-building; while undoubtedly fiction, this can hardly be called a novel.

[8] Although I didn't know it when I first read it, Eddings had intended *The Belgariad* to be a trilogy; it was divided into a quintet for reasons of length at the insistence of editor, Lester del Rey. See 'Prime U.S. Beef: David Eddings Interviewed by Stan Nicholls', *Interzone* No. 85 (July 1994), pp.25 30.

[9] Comprising twenty-six 25-minute episodes, *Doctor Who: The Key to Time* was released as a DVD box set by BBC Warner in 2002.

[10] I've spent enough time in the academic world to know too well, and to some extent to have internalised, the prejudices against fantasy. Of course there is a vast amount of bad fantasy published: but the notion that fantasy

is inherently inferior to realism is a provincial delusion, bizarre when considering literature in its full historical range. See Tolkien: "Much that [is nowadays called] 'serious' literature is no more than play under a glass roof by the side of a municipal swimming-bath. Fairy-stories may invent monsters that fly the air or dwell in the deep, but at least they do not try to escape from heaven or the sea". (op. cit., p.56).

Did you ask any good questions today, child?
Science fiction and the argumentative narrative

Farah Mendlesohn

The title of this chapter is taken from a Jewish tradition: it is the question you ask a child on his return from school, the idea being to inculcate a critical approach to the world. This approach extends up to, and includes, the word of God, which is not to be accepted as sealed, perfect, but is to be haggled over, argued. After all, He told us that after Moses smashed the ten commandments, He would never again give His word directly.[1] People would have to peer through a glass darkly to discern His intentions. And even then they would probably argue. Biblical history shows very little in the way of absolute obedience to the Lord; time and again, the average cry of an Old Testament prophet was 'Why me?' or 'You must be kidding!' In the Jewish view of the universe, the world is unfair and all you can do is argue your corner. Science fiction – as writers such as Isaac Asimov and Robert Silverberg have noted – is a very Jewish literature.

Elsewhere I have written that while fantasy wants to make the world succumb to moral imperatives (the dispossessed princess is reinstalled, the bad god dies, the hero gets the sword – even the subversive fantasies of authors such as John Crowley, Elizabeth Hand, or Caroline Stevermer operate within these expectations), science fiction wants the world to be just (*The Cambridge Companion to Science Fiction*, 2003). It wants it to have rules, so that we know if we press this lever then this cog will turn, this engine will fire, and the rocket will take off. It also wants to know that there are loop holes, rules that can be twisted. And it wants *you* to know that if you break the rules you will die. If you are a duffer you won't just drown; there is a good chance you will drown, freeze to death in the vacuum of open space, starve for ignoring the imperatives of the market (or the logics of communitarianism), or be unable to breathe because you forgot to check your oxygen mask before leaving for work this morning. The encyclopedist and critic John Clute has called this "making the universe storyable" (*The Encyclopedia of Fantasy*, 1997, p.899).

In this way the narrative arcs of science fiction (sf) simultaneously strive to be both cosy and disorienting. Much of the critical attention to sf focuses on the genre's disorienting aspects, and I will come to that, but I want to demonstrate the degree to which questions are at the heart of the sf 'story' by discussing its cosiness.

Tom Godwin's 'The Cold Equations' (1954) is one of the most discussed short stories in the field. It is an example of what is popularly known as 'hard sf' (one of many subgenres of the field). It relies on a combination of engineering and physics for its plot, but old-fashioned gallantry for its emotional impact.

A man flying a small spacecraft to an alien planet discovers a stowaway on board. What should he do? Here are the factors in his choice:

- He is on his way with a vaccine to save the planet from disease.
- In order to make the greatest speed, the ship is stripped to the bones, its weight calculated to the micro-gramme.
- In order to cut back on weight, there is only enough fuel for the weight of the ship as recorded on departure.
- The stowaway is a girl (actually a young woman, but she is portrayed as very young) and she wanted to visit her brother.

The debate that has raged around this story (see Huntingdon, James and Cramer) is about the pilot's decision to eject (or 'space') the young woman.

To non-sf readers the structure of this story may appear tedious.

The man and the young woman go through a series of questions in which the man explains to the woman the physics of space flight, of fuel load, etc., etc. To each objection she offers, he has an answer. Finally, the young woman accepts that the needs of the many outweigh the desires of the few. Teary-eyed, after a talk on video with her brother, the young woman steps into space.

At this point it's useful to know that the stowaway was originally a young man. The editor of *Astounding Science Fiction*, John W. Campbell, persuaded Godwin to change the sex of the protagonist precisely in order to enhance tension between emotion and intellect. The result, as a number of commentators have pointed out, is a rather duplicitous story because the ship is *full* of things that could have been stripped to release the weight of the young woman. That this was missed by contemporary and by first-time readers (myself included) is due to the structure of the story: the question and answer prose falls into the rhythm of catechism. Ironically, it persuades the reader *not* to interrogate the story, not, in fact, to resist the universe. The reliance on the rules of the cosmos creates a cosiness in which humanity becomes passive.

Yet the question-narrative of the sf tale can be enormously powerful. The basic question of the sf narrative is "What if ...?" It can be about engineering: what if you need to build a railway on a planet which has miniature volcanoes erupting every couple of hundred yards? [2] It can be philosophical: what happens if you introduce Christianity to a culture with no belief in original sin? [3] Or introduce Christianity to three species who already share a trinitarian symbiosis and in which the death of one member of the trinity is supposed to lead to the suicide of the other two? [4] Or wonder how five intelligent species stranded on a single planet might get on? [5] Or it can question the impact of new physics on social relations: What happens if a quantum event opens up a new universe on your doorstep, and the things coming through are doing strange things to your society and your body? [6] In each case, there is an assumption, not that human beings can fix anything, but that the relationship between humanity and the universe is that between engineer and environment. It is a fierce, dialectical relationship and it is conducted through a four-note strategy that I have (impertinently) called FULL SF. [7] This strategy can be summed up as:

Dissonance is a useful shorthand for what Darko Suvin famously termed "cognitive estrangement" or, "the thing which is different" (*Metamorphoses of Science Fiction*, 1975). Most modern sf (anything written much after Robert A. Heinlein began writing and John W. Campbell started editing, around 1940) contains more than one "thing which is different". The aim is to simultaneously disorient the reader, and to bring them further into the world by coaxing them to accept *as natural* something other than what they know. At its most brutal, this can be Faster Than Light travel (FTL), a convenient device that allows authors to link planets and, like the mobile phone, changes the dynamics of society. This dissonance generates the structuring questions; what can you do when another planet is merely days away? Well, invasion narratives to begin with. And trade. And disease vectors. And the speed of fashion will probably increase. And throw into that a very long-lived culture with a moral imperative to have as many children as possible. With a belief that men are property to be traded. Suddenly the what-ifs acquire huge complexity and possibilities. Conventional plot narratives – boy meets girl – take on new complexity when the question is 'what does girl need to do in order to secure the dower price for her boy, without alienating the two boys she's already bought?' And how does she decide which of her boys gets to sire/parent? And does a sire necessarily parent? Best genes aren't always best father material.

Once you've set up your *Dissonance* then you have to *Rupture* it. These ruptures, too, generate questions which generate narrative: our Hero is busy working out how to purchase the boy of her dreams, when the family business is undermined by a brand new technology and she has to work out how to apply the new tech in profitable ways; or aliens invade and they decide that all men are oppressed and it's their duty to liberate them – suddenly her boy goes off to university and half her workforce leave; or virtual uploads mean she can live for ever and the need for an heir disappears. Take your choice. You can have a single *Rupture* or you can inflict on your hero one *Rupture* after another after another.

From there we move to *Resolution*. This is frequently the least satisfactory part of a sf narrative, because if the narrative drive in sf is towards change, almost any conventional ending – falling in love, making lots of money, finding out who was trying to destroy your country – is rather static. It's an *answer* in a genre which is much more interested in the questions. Which takes us to my last note in the melody – *Consequence.* This is controversial because this is simply my opinion; the idea has not been out there long enough to be either taken up or dismissed. A successful sf text needs to extend beyond the end of the book. The best way to see this is to consider the narrative trajectory of sf's kissin' cousin, the futuristic thriller. At the end of the thriller, the bomb is defused, the plague cured, the asteroid deflected. Everything goes back to normal until the next *Rupture.* In *good* science there is rarely a guarantee that a 'solution' in these terms is likely to be found. Science fiction solutions are more likely to involve a radical change in direction, what John Clute has called a "slingshot" ending (p.875) which opens up yet *more* questions: we don't deflect the asteroid so we all climb in a space-ship instead; the disease kills millions: we have to deal with a depleted work force, crop shortages and the collapse in infrastructure; or the disease kills millions but those who survive have been transformed into light-wave intelligences. Faster-than-light travel changes the trade routes so dramatically that empires collapse, former metropolises turn into ghost towns and there are huge waves of immigration. So that there is an oddly recursive structure: most modern sf begins after the last rupture, and ends on the cusp (or just beyond the apex) of the next rupture. At the end of an sf novel is always the Big Question: *What happens next?*

Now let's turn to a few texts to see all of this in practice. These are not intended to represent typical sf texts. There is as much sloppy thinking in sf as there is in any branch of writing, but I have tried to choose a few really excellent examples in a number of the different sub-genres of sf.

Space operas are big, romantic adventures which do not always take place in space. They tend to juxtapose an individual swashbuckler against the huge canvasses of the galaxy. Their prose ranges from the merely lurid to the gorgeously over-wrought – as iron gates can be over-wrought.

Until very recently, the idea that space opera might be part of the interrogative dynamic of sf would have caused most critics and fans to laugh.[8] This began to change in the 1990s when the New Space Opera emerged. The author most associated with the New Space Opera is Iain M. Banks (who writes mainstream 'weird' fiction without the middle M). Banks' Culture novels (listed in the works cited) ask one very simple question: what would be the sources of conflict in a post-scarcity society? And this is a society in which *nothing* is scarce. Travel is free: hop on board a ship which is inhabited/driven by an artificial intelligence. Change your sex. Alter your hormones or the chemicals in your body with just a thought. Disappear from the world and spend your life studying the gas-bag intelligences of another planet, never seeing another member of your species again. What is left to cause the conflict which generations of critics have told us is at the heart of literature?

Banks' secondary question, the one that drives the sequence is: 'what happens when utopia meets The Other?' A question present in Thomas More's classic *Utopia*, and noted by a number of Utopian scholars such as Tom Moylan. Can utopia only exist at the expense of its neighbours? Once convinced that it is right, the Culture has both to defend itself from incursions and, needing to create a buffer-zone around itself, needs to expand. The Culture series opens with *Consider Phlebas*, a utopian novel told from the point of view of someone who wants to bring the utopia down. The other books in the series interrogate the various ways in which the Culture seeks to embed itself. In *Player of Games*, the Culture sends a missionary to undermine a society whose rather unpleasant 'meritocracy' is based on an annual gaming competition which *just happens* to reinforce class and gender prejudices, but the question that it asks of the reader is to consider what embedded prejudices structure both the Culture and our own societies. In *Use of Weapons*, the Culture hires a non-Culture mercenary to intervene in the governments of other societies and challenges the 'intervention' protocols of the western world. *Look to Windward* contemplates the trauma endured by those so used, and by the societies which have been incorporated into the Culture. My personal favourite, *Excession*, sees a faction within the Culture make use of an intrusion they do not understand to deflect an uprising which they themselves have triggered in order to undermine it early. There is a rather surprising consistency to the question at the heart of these books: how is a society defined, in terms of those with which it deals, and the ways in which it eschews responsibility for its own actions?

To deviate for a moment, in the 1960s Marion Zimmer Bradley began a series of novels set on the planet of Darkover. In the planet's past, weapons had been devised that were so frightening that the Compact was signed: only weapons which brought the wielder into as much danger as the target were permitted (so swords, but no bows). In his Culture novels, Banks chose to consider a society which wanted to keep its hands clean, but to do so constructed a narrow definition of violence. [9] Bradley chose to construct one in which getting one's hands bloody was considered the ethically purer approach. Both Bradley and Banks were asking questions not about the nature of violence, but about its context. If you change what it is socially acceptable to *do*, what happens? The answer (as so often in sf) is that humans are persistent and ingenious primates. [10]

Reading Banks' novels also takes us back to issues I raised early on: who are sf stories about? Within each of his novels are small human concerns. In the midst of utopia people continue to screw up their lives. Banks' fictions usually use these micro-stories as distractions from the main event. His real 'stories' are about a large political entity coming head to head with the cold justice of the universe. Mostly, the political entity wins, but the universe gets its own back on the innocent bystanders.

One of the problems with utopias is that, like the catechism of 'The Cold Equations' they frequently delegitimise interrogation. As long as the surface remains undisturbed they are convincing, poke below that surface and they collapse. In *Triton* (1975) Samuel R. Delany challenged the idea that the purpose of utopia is to make individuals happy. In *Triton* (subtitled *An Ambiguous Heterotopia*), Bron indulges his desire for, "life, liberty and the pursuit of misery", while we get to see how other people go about asking questions and making social constructs. Small questions about childcare blossom into co-ops based on sexual affinity groups, or age phalanxes. Safety is protected by the construction of an unlicensed zone. Gender identity is protected by choice – no need for ideological and essentialist constructions when you can walk in as a small white woman and leave as a large black man.

For many sf writers the importance of questions is intimately linked with the ownership of knowledge; it is no coincidence that one of the themes that crops up repeatedly in sf is the persistence of memory. There is a great deal of post-nuclear holocaust fiction, and large numbers of generation ship narratives (people get in a space ship and expect their great grandchildren to make it to the new planet). In almost all of these memory is faded and distorted. The three great classics are Robert A. Heinlein's 1951 *Orphans of the Sky* (although the original stories were written in the 1940s), Walter J. Miller's *A Canticle for Leibowitz* (1959) and Sylvia Engdahl's *Heritage of the Star* (1972). What these texts have in common is that within the constructed societies questions have become anathema, catechism is the rule, myth has taken over. In each – and in the many other books written in this vein [11] – it is the ability to question that breaks down cultural stasis. One way to think about this is to reconsider George Santayana's comment, "those who cannot remember the past are condemned to repeat it". These books are constructed around the ethos that *those who cannot question the past, are condemned to drift blindly into the future.* The slingshot ending is triggered precisely by the decision to keep asking awkward questions.

In the 1950s futurists were confident that they could predict the development of modern technology. It was assumed that techno-logical (and political) development was linear. By the 1990s it was clear to everyone that this couldn't be true: humans were living through a 'singularity', an event horizon beyond which present models of the future cease to give reliable or accurate answers. As the sf author Stephen Baxter has pointed out in his article in *Foundation* 98 (2006), this is by no means the first singularity: a farm girl in northern England in 1780 could not have predicted that her daughters would work in an industry that barely existed. In 1950 many of the towns of the 1970s were farmland and fields (and had been for at least 2000 years).

The first hint of the next singularity came with cyberpunk. William Gibson's 1980 novel *Neuromancer* envisaged a future in which humans could link directly to computers, could move about inside a virtual world. And this was *before* the unexpected appearance of personal computers on people's desks. [12] Once small mainframes, and then personal computers spread out, then the most urgent questions began to revisit the relationship of humans to technology, old Marxist ideas about the enslavement of humans to technological processes [13] combined with more recent cultural theory which presumes the relationship to be more argumentative.

Although we have removed many of the pressures that shape species (at least in the west), new circumstances generate new evolutionary holes for our descendants to squeeze through. [14] One of the dominant questions of sf has been, if we are *not* the pinnacle of evolution what comes next? Many of these new circumstances are ones we have created: the definition of 'civilization' may one day include the ability to shape our own genetic future.

In *Natural History*, Justina Robson tests the edge of humanity as her genetically altered Forged go out into the world with new bodies and minds whose form dictates function, a radical revisioning of the idea of 'adaptable' humanity. But as ever with modern sf, the questions do not stop with departure. The Forged are human so they in turn ask questions, challenge the Bauhaus ideology of their progenitors and wonder whether the universe was made for them, or they for the universe, an old riff on the notion of God made new. Humans, oldstyle humans, are left behind in this future: the singularity they have created is one they cannot predict or follow. [15]

Some singularities are more plausible than others: humans have been asking for several centuries whether there is anyone out there, and it's beginning to look as if the answer is in the negative, or at least, our neighbours are so far away that our wagon trains can't get there. Writers do still speculate about first contact however, and although there have been huge ideological shifts in first contact novels (which used to focus mostly on empire or invasion) the fundamental question remains the same: are we unique?

The writer to take this on most recently is Karen Traviss. Her *Wess'har* series (*City of Pearl*, *Crossing the Line*, *The World Before* and *Matriarch*) considers what happens when humans come across a species that doesn't think humans are so very special – not even as enemies. For Traviss, the crucial issue is not why humans believe they are so special, but the consequences of doing so. The belief itself she posits, is sociobiological: a consequence of being both prey and predator, it means that humans need the ability to continually renegotiate what is 'legitimate' prey (not just as food, but as a resource generally), so that at times some species become reclassified as 'pets' while some of our fellow humans are reclassified as 'prey'.[16] Traviss uses the wess'har to expose the lies we tell ourselves: to the wess'har, all living things are people: exploitation of other people is *ipso facto* wrong.

Like Robson, Traviss argues for a relationship between form and function but it is one that goes much deeper: humans are aggressive because we are over-crowded primates, both prey and predator. We have status structures constructed around display and challenge, sexual relations that are about power. The wess'har are non-prey, non-predator herd animals, vegetarians who mate one female to a number of males, who must swap genetic material to ensure good health and who change status according to scent signals. Traviss succeeds in making a story of the politicised nature of storytelling itself; humans write stories of origin and uniqueness and of manifest destiny; the wess'har write stories of co-operation and community.

The clash between these perspectives becomes the drive of the story, but it is the asking of questions which is the narrative: Shan Frankland, protagonist and hero, environmental police officer and now refugee on a foreign planet, is the interrogator of both her own homeworld's policies and those of the wess'har and their cousins from their own planet – for the wess'har too are in the midst of a sociobiological struggle. As each question is asked, and each conflict 'resolved' the future looks ever more uncertain. Singularities occur at every turn: human scientists dissect a baby bezerji and trigger their own extinction; the wess'har call for help from their older cousins, and lose control of the plot; the issenj' ask for help with their population problems, and the wess'har begin a process which might itself trigger a genocidal war. With each turn the neat answers of conventional narrative shrivel and die.

Sf is distinctive as a form of literature for a number of reasons; its protagonists' focus is frequently on the macro-world. While literature from outside the genre tends to focus on relationships between individuals *against a background of* ... (take your pick of Hollywood trailers), sf tends to reverse that.

Science fiction tells stories of the collapse of empires, first contact, new technologies against a background of the personal, and it does this precisely by asking questions. Driving all of this is an attitude to the world which asks: if I only had a big enough screwdriver could I take the back off the world? If I could speak to God, could I ask the big enough question? Could I take that mythical lever, and move the universe? The question narrative forces the story to extend into the future: however much a tale may be wrapped up, the world as it ends is not the world as it began. Changes have been made and we are all sitting in the sling waiting for the catapult to launch us into Consequence. In the end the question, and not the answer, is the romance of science fiction.

Notes

[1] While ultra-orthodox Jews may seem 'extreme' to liberals, the same ultra-orthodox would regard Christian and Islamic fundamentalism as heretical because of its presumptuousness.

[2] In Colin Kapp's 'The Railways Up On Cannis', the Unorthodox Engineers realise that the only place a volcano never erupts, is where there has been a volcano. So they plant mines, create their own volcanoes, saw off the top of the cooled structure and use the now dead volcanoes as pillars on which they rest the railway tracks. *New Worlds* (1959).

[3] In Harry Harrison's 'The Streets of Ashkelon' the indigenous peoples crucify the missionary in order to check the bible is true. *New Worlds* (1962), pp.49-63.

[4] In John Barnes' *The Sin of Origin* 'remnants' take the message of re-birth in Christ as authority to form new trinities, which their world regards as both heretical and a threat to the social order (Congdon & Weed, 1988).

[5] David Brin's *Heaven's Reach* (Tor, 1998)

[6] *Light* by M. John Harrison, in which the only thing stranger than what the universe does to you, are the things you choose to do to yourself in the strange belief that what you do matters and that the universe cares (Orion/Gollancz, 2002).

[7] The term has been adapted from John Clute's conceptualisation of the FULL FANTASY which he elaborates on in *The Encyclopedia of Fantasy* (Orbit, 1997), p.339.

[8] Many of the 'big names' in science fiction criticism are independent scholars. Some, like Damon Knight, James Blish, M. John Harrison and John Clute were/are authors, but many others began as fans and went onto produce highly-respected review columns for the genre's trade magazines. Current practioners include David Langford, Russell Letson, Cheryl Morgan and Niall Harrison.

[9] The issue of what *is* violence continually vexes pacifists. The Quakers, for example, are uncomfortable with sanctions which might generate famine.

¹⁰ This notion is rather crucial to modern science fiction. Nothing annoys sf readers more than *stupid* protagonists, but by this I mean stupid as humans rather than stupid as individuals. In Jeanne DuPrau's *City of Ember* (a book written for children) an underground society does not recycle, has potatoes for its main crop, has only one clock (which is wind up) and the secret of exit is written down only once – on paper. And when the children find the escape tunnel they do it using candles and matches left for them in the tunnel. Think about those things. And then think about the ingenuity of people living in barrios and rubbish dumps, on inhospitable islands, in the arctic wastes (Random House, 2003).

¹¹ See also, Carol Emshwiller, *The Mount: A Novel* (Small Beer Press, 2002); Sheri Tepper, *Family Tree* (HarperCollins, 1997).

¹² A personal anecdote: there is an episode of *To the Manor Born* in which Richard (the head of the company which has bought the manor) is showing the ex-lady of the house, Audrey, the new computer which has arrived on his desk. It's a singularity moment. This small box can track his entire business. Re-watching it is like watching the first human strike the first flame.

¹³ See Donna Haraway's 'Manifesto for Cyborgs' lauded as a hugely original insight, it is actually a recapitulation of Marx's theory of alienation of labour. Haraway also doesn't know what a cyborg is (it's a human being who has been enhanced by machinery directly implanted in the body, a person who is a mixture of organic and inorganic parts – someone with a pacemaker is a cyborg).

¹⁴ The ability to cope with too much sugar and fat in our diet may well prove to be an evolutionary pressure now that diet-related illness and death is affecting the pre-pubertal.

¹⁵ This notion of humans left behind is another of the central what ifs. Greg Egan has fun with the idea in *Schild's Ladder* (Orion/Gollancz, 2002). Ken MacLeod reckons we should destroy the superhuman *now* before it can destroy us in a competition for living space in *The Cassini Division* (Orbit, 1998).

¹⁶ Currently, British 'missionaries' are trying to persuade the Chinese not to eat cats and dogs, while in America it is perfectly legal to test drugs on convicts.

Bibliography

Iain M. Banks, *Player of Games* (Macmillan, 1988); *Use of Weapons* (Orbit, 1990); *Excession* (Orbit, 1996); *Consider Phlebas* (Macmillan, 1997).

John Barnes, *Sin of Origin* (Congdon & Weed, 1988).

Stephen Baxter, 'Children of the Urban Singularity: The Industrial Landscape of Britain and the Science Fiction Imagination' in *Foundation* 98 (2006).

Marion Zimmer Bradley, *Two to Conquer* (Arrow Books, 1982).

David Brin, *Heaven's Reach* (Bantam Spectra, 1998).

Lois McMaster Bujold, *Warriors' Apprentice*.

Kathryn Cramer, 'Hard Science Fiction' in *The Cambridge Companion to Science Fiction*, eds. Edward James & Farah Mendlesohn (Cambridge University Press, 2003), pp.186-96.

John Clute and John Grant, *The Encyclopedia of Fantasy* (Orbit, 1997).

Samuel R. Delany, *Triton: An Ambiguous Heterotopia* (Bantam, 1976).

Jeanne DuPrau, *City of Ember* (Random House, 2003).

Greg Egan, *Schild's Ladder* (Orion/Gollancz, 2002).

Carol Emshwiller, *The Mount: A Novel* (Small Beer Press, 2002).

Sylvia Engdahl, *Heritage of the Star* (Gollancz, 1972).

Tom Godwin, 'The Cold Equations' in *Astounding Science Fiction* (1954), pp.62-84.

Donna Haraway, 'A Cyborg Manifesto: Science, Technology, and Socialist-Feminism in the Late Twentieth Century' in *Simians, Cyborgs and Women: The Reinvention of Nature*, ed. Donna Haraway (Routledge, 1991), pp.149-81.

Harry Harrison, 'The Streets of Ashkelon' in *New Worlds* (1962), pp.49-63.

M. John Harrison, *The Centauri Device* (1975); *Light* (Orion/Gollancz, 2002).

Robert A. Heinlein, *Orphans of the Sky* (Gollancz, 1966).

John Huntington, *Rationalizing Genius* (Routledge, 1989).

Edward James, *Science Fiction in the 20th Century* (Oxford University Press, 1994).

Edward James and Farah Mendlesohn, eds., *Cambridge Companion to Science Fiction* (Cambridge University Press, 2003).

Colin Kapp, 'The Railways up on Cannis' in *New Worlds* (1959).

Locus, August 2003. New Space Opera special issue.

Ken MacLeod, *The Cassini Division* (Orbit, 1998).

Walter J. Miller, *A Canticle for Leibowitz* (Bantam, 1959).

Thomas Moore, *Utopia*.

Tom Moylan, *Scraps of the Untainted Sky: Science Fiction, Utopia, Dystopia* (Westview Press, 1997).

Alasdair Reynolds, *Revelation Space* (Gollancz, 2000).

Justina Robson, *Natural History* (Macmillan, 2003).

Charles Stross, *Accelerando* (Tor, 2005).

Darko Suvin, *Metamorphoses of Science Fiction* (Yale University Press, 1979).

Sheri Tepper, *Family Tree* (HarperCollins, 1997).

Karen Traviss, *City of Pearl* (Eos, 2004); *Crossing the Line* (Eos, 2004); *The World Before* (Eos, 2005); *Matriarch* (Eos, 2006).

David Weber, *Honor of the Queen* (BaenBooks, 1994)

8

Telling Tales out of School

Mary Hammond

The Beginning

In the Spring of 1995, when I was a second-year undergraduate, I experienced something in the nature of a revelation. I remember the moment clearly. I was sitting at my kitchen table trying to write an essay on John Donne, and I was in tears. This was not in itself unusual. I was a mature student for whom the road into Higher Education had wound through a range of careers including sheep farming, art school, professional authorship and full-time motherhood. I was 35 years old and my partner and two children and I were struggling along on one modest income just so I could have this opportunity. This was, I knew, probably my last chance to prove to the world that I could actually stick at something, and if the truth be told it wasn't going all that well; my first year essays had gained me pedestrian marks at best and I was bumping along on a lowly 2:2 average. English literature, the one thing I had always felt most sure about in my life, had already unseated me and was galloping off into the distance where the smart people lived, leaving me groping around with the losers in its wake. Tears had already figured fairly heavily in my academic life to date.

This year, however, the pressure had been cranked up a notch; this year every mark counted towards my degree and – just to make sure we didn't get comfortable – the essay questions were harder. I had been wrestling with the Donne essay for two days and I was behind schedule. It was Monday, and I had two more essays (Chaucer and Modernism, neither of them a walk in the park) due by Thursday afternoon. The kids would be home from school in less than an hour, after which time thought patterns would necessarily stray away from metaphysics towards baked beans and ballet lessons and my working day would be effectively over. The panic was bubbling up under my breastbone.

I remember staring at the piles of books scattered over the table in front of me, my carefully compiled sheaves of hand-written notes, and the typed instructions on How to Write an Essay thoughtfully provided by my department. "Make a Plan," said Step One. Well, I'd done that on Saturday. And two days later it was still as compelling as a dead fish. "Structure is crucial," said Step Two. But the structure of what? How can you structure something that doesn't exist? I sensed that somewhere in the relationship between all the critical texts I'd gathered and all the notes I'd made about the poems lay my essay. But I was too novice an alchemist to know the formula that would give it life. The Wizards of Academia still held the answer to that particular mystery, and (essay-writing tips notwithstanding) they clearly weren't telling.

Part of my frustration came from the fact that I really ought to have known this stuff. After all, at some point way back in the mists of time (around the late 1970s, which is approximately the same thing) I had studied John Donne before. Indeed, before me on the kitchen table lay a cracked and yellowed copy of my old A Level text *Metaphysical Lyrics and Poems of the Seventeenth Century*, each Donne poem passionately annotated in black fountain pen (my feeble attempt at sophistication – or perhaps at alchemy of a different sort), complete with my personal mnemonics and all the signs of a long-forgotten narrative of my teenage thought processes. The annotations were no help whatsoever now (what had I meant by "Chosen few – angels", when I'd written it beside *Holy Sonnet No. 3*? Why had I written "Rubbish" at the top of *The Extasie*?), but I suppose I hoped that their enthusiasm might inspire me.

I looked harder at the annotations, struck by something. They weren't decipherable to me now, I realised, but they *did* tell a story; in fact they told several stories. On a micro level they were part of the story of that particular qualification, the concentration and despair and euphoria which I can no longer remotely grasp; the slaved-for and briefly prized Grade 'A' certificate which I have long since misplaced. On another level, too, they were part of my own life story, the one that had led me from an evening class in A Level English Literature to a place at Art School, and then to my first full-time job as a writer and researcher, working on mass-market paperbacks for an American book packager. In this case, I reflected, the alchemy had worked. Writing A Level and Art School essays had helped me to write novels. The sheer practice, the flexing of my creative muscles, the building of my confidence (and, it has to be said, the arrogance of youth), had led me to believe that I could bid for a competitive contract alongside far more experienced fiction writers. And I had been right. I had got the contract. I had spent four years co-writing historical novels and learning about how stories worked.

Somewhere, my instincts were telling me now, in that pile of notes and critical writings on John Donne, was my essay. Those instincts had been developed writing stories. Why not approach this essay like a story? Why not try reversing the process? The tears stopped. I got suddenly excited. *An essay is not a story*, I heard my budding Academic-self intone disapprovingly. *It takes rational thought, not instinct or inspiration. You will fail. You will end up writing journalism for the tabloid press.* So what, my storytelling side answered back? I have a deadline and ten pages to fill, just as I used to do. And at least this way I'll get it done. I picked up my pen. To hell with university, I thought. To hell with John Donne, for that matter. Scarlett-like, I gritted my teeth, wrote the essay question at the top of a new page and muttered: "As God is my witness, I will never cry over an essay again." And I never have.

What are the most important components of storytelling, I thought, casting my mind back a few years and starting a new list on my dead-fish of an essay plan? Conflict, of course. A cracking plot. Characters. Relationships. Good dialogue. Why should any of that be different for an academic essay? Of course, *some* elements would necessarily be different. I wasn't likely to get very far pretending that Donne could speak for himself or that I'd known him personally ("I caught up with John over a couple of martinis after church. 'So tell me, John,' I said. 'What is your response to the critics who think *The Extasie* is rubbish?'"). But literal parallels aside, isn't persuasion just another rhetorical strategy, like creating a credible world out of pen and ink? Does effective persuasion make an academic essay true, in any essential, irrefutable sense? No, I decided, it doesn't. Not in the Arts, anyway. It makes it persuasive, that's all. Just like a good story.

Conflict, then. Let us start there. Not a problem for me really, as, being from Yorkshire and by nature an argumentative sort, I like a good fight. Among my piles of notes drawn from the critics, I realised, true to nature I had spent quite a lot of time copying down quotations with which I violently disagreed (another glimmer of light dawned: that "Rubbish!" written beside *The Extasie* in 1979 began to make sense). I leafed through them and chose one, the one with which I disagreed most violently. I wrote that quote at the top of the page thus: 'So-and-so has argued that such-and-such is true.' I had my first line. I then wrote. 'This suggests that such-and such is also true.' I had my second line. Beneath it I wrote: "However, this assumption ignores one of the most common but least critically evaluated tropes in Donne's poetry ... etc." I had my third line. And I had both conflict (my disagreement with the critic, signalled from the very first lines) and the beginnings of a plot (if X happened and Y happened, then Z had to happen in consequence. E.M. Forster would have been proud of me.) I had characters (me, the critics and Donne) and relationships (the fact that Donne couldn't speak for himself and the critics and I were free to maul each other over him). I had dialogue (the juxtaposing of the critics' arguments with mine). I had a beginning (setting up my argument), a middle (amassing evidence) and an end, complete with narrative resolution (this critic is talking crap and I've just proved it). Above all, I was enjoying myself.

The essay wrote itself. It really did. More so than any story I have ever written (which is probably why I ended up being an academic and not a novelist). I was hard put to squeeze it into two thousand words. Excited by my discovery of the essay-as-story, I couldn't wait to try it on Chaucer. The next day I found another critic I disagreed with, and wrote about how widely he'd missed the point about *The House of Fame*. The day before the deadline, I viciously saw off an equally erroneous analysis of D.H. Lawrence. I honed my new craft with each attempt, discovering, for example, that if I wrote the essay title at the top of each new page it kept the theme to the forefront of my mind, much as I used to write the central theme of my novels onto post-its and stick them to the keyboard of my Underwood. I realised, too, that the notes I took while reading were a kind of writer's journal, in which my unconscious mind was pre-selecting the bits that would eventually be relevant, and I just had to trust it to know what it was doing.

Finally, I proofread the essays, printed them, handed them in, and waited. I didn't expect to do any better than I'd done in my first year, but I felt incredibly liberated by the fact that I had enjoyed writing all three of them, and that I felt ready to take on the next three in the summer.

What I thought I'd done was simply to cure my writer's block. What I'd actually done was to embark on a whole new career.

The Middle

I was stunned when all three essays got Firsts, and the Chaucer one led to an invitation to apply for the Medieval Literature MA. I didn't accept in the end, but I did graduate with a high First overall, opted for the Modern Literature MA and finished off with a PhD. I was having so much fun writing what I had come to think of as 'stories with scholarly themes' that I didn't want to stop.

I began to publish some of my essays, and somehow became an academic. I am still surprised that I have become an academic, because what I feel I really am is someone who makes their living by writing stories. The essay-as-story trick didn't go away; in fact it blossomed, and as I progressed from answering pre-set questions to thinking up research questions of my own, I realised it had become as much about subject matter as technique. My choice of MA dissertation (popular literature in 1910), my PhD (reading habits in England 1880-1914), and my eventual specialism (English publishing history and readers in the 19th and early 20th centuries) were largely determined by the stories I had heard while growing up, and by the gaps in my knowledge of my family history.

It was while I was still an undergraduate taking assiduous notes in yet another Modernism class that I realised why I kept on taking those sorts of classes, and what I might want to specialise in as a postgraduate. It was because Modernism classes centred on the historical period that my grandparents had inhabited in their youth that I returned to them again and again. I remembered my grandparents very well; their worldview, their stories, their house and all its contents were formative parts of my childhood. I wanted new insights into their world, a world which had ended in 1988 with my grandmother's death at the age of 95. But the Modernism classes were, I realised, baffling and frustrating. None of the books we studied in those classes had been on my grandparents' bookshelves. None of the Modernist concerns about social decay and vulgar populism and social miscegenation seemed connected to their daily lives. Born in the early 1890s, they had lived through the First World War (my grandfather had been at both Ypres and the Somme, my grandmother liberated from domestic service and launched into a new career as a tram conductress) and married in the year of the Armistice. When I was little they showed me spent German shell casings made into pincushions and played me music hall songs on their gramophone. They sort of believed in God, but not at all in the Church, and they were quietly supportive of the monarchy. They had brought up three children between the wars in a two-up two-down terraced house with an outside toilet, and had lost their elder child to rheumatic fever. Even when they moved to a posh, new red brick house in suburbia they continued keeping chickens in the back yard, and growing their own fruit and vegetables. Autumn for me still means the smell of hundreds of drying apples wrinkling quietly on newspaper on every available surface of the kitchen and scullery; the red rawness of women's hands as they sit around a table, basins in laps, slicing and salting runner beans for the winter in a gentle ebb and flow of neighbourly storytelling; the sizzle of bacon fat being dropped onto damp coals to coax the first recalcitrant fire of the year; the yeasty waft of new bread rising in a coal-fired oven.

Modernist concerns were not part of my grandparents' lives, though they inhabited that same historical moment. I looked in vain in the pages of Woolf and Joyce and Yeats and Eliot for a glimmer of insight into my family's past. I tried getting my mother to read Lawrence's wonderful First World War short story 'Tickets, Please', naively believing that she would find it interesting. She didn't. In fact she strongly suggested that I keep it away from my grandmother, who was likely to be offended by its suggestion that tram conductresses sometimes thought about sex.

I even tried looking further afield, browsing among the catalogues of other literature degrees looking for something familiar which might tempt me to do an MA elsewhere. I didn't find it. The period 1880-1935 meant Modernism or War or both, and that was that. So I decided to find out on my own what else was going on in that period, why Modernist authors had not been on my grandparents' bookshelves, what they had read, how much it had cost, and what it said about them. My choice of MA dissertation and PhD thesis sprang, quite simply, from the desire to tell their story, to understand my own history, to fill in the blanks I found in university courses. I became a book historian, really, because my grandmother would have remained more of a mystery to me if I hadn't.

I believe many academic careers and many academic specialisms in literature start that way, though I have been disagreed with on more than one occasion by colleagues who maintain that all their work is objective. I know for a fact that much of mine isn't. I have learned to write in a register which pushes the 'me writing' to the background, but the family stories and the subjective concerns are still there. Objectivity is often a smokescreen – there are surely many feminist, Marxist, queer or post-colonialist scholars in literature departments across Britain who, like me, have not entirely chosen their specialisms at random. In many cases we are personally involved, and we want to tell our stories. And while to a point the declaration of a particular political position based on skin colour or accent or gender or whatever can be an acceptable way of authenticating ourselves in academia, stories are not quite what is expected in an academic essay. Rightly so, up to a point: a subjective opinion alone does not constitute evidence. But the wholesale rejection of personal investment in the academic stories we tell, and of the many rhetorical strategies shared by essay-writers and storytellers, is perhaps a little unrealistic.

There's a story behind it, of course, a story filled with class and gender struggle, with oppression and revolution, and with a star-spangled cast of characters, but it must remain merely a sub-plot here. Suffice it to say that the study of literature at university level in England is relatively new, having started just before the First World War. And very insecure it was too: a fledgling discipline, afraid of being booed off the stage by the scientists. As a result, it worked extra hard at being clever and rational and quantifiable. It focused on books and poetry and plays with a high esteem factor and turned its nose up at the merely best selling. It produced sophisticated methodologies for interrogating and understanding literature and began to assume that authors were the last people to know anything significant about what they produced. In England, throughout much of the 20th century, 'Literature' was considered the product of inspired genius, and scholarly research into it the province of a highly-educated elite. Some extraordinary individuals were able to do both, of course, but never on the same page.

Things were slightly different in American universities, for obvious reasons. A meritocracy has a different relationship to popular success than a class-bound society based on hereditary power, such as Britain. And – curiously but not coincidentally – American academics are far less troubled by the confessional or anecdotal in essays. For them, the crossover between the creative and the scholarly is not viewed as though it were an outbreak of bird 'flu. But in Britain the insecurity remained – and in some senses still remains.

What relevance has this sub-plot to my story? Well, through its very opposition it underlines my main theme, which is one of continuity between the urge to tell stories and the way we make sense of the world, whether in an essay or a moment of self-understanding. Finding out as a postgraduate that the institutional opposition between 'creative' and 'scholarly' writing is a historical construction and not a natural law has helped me to see the two untidy 'halves' of my own life, the writerly and the scholarly (separated but also guiltily brought together by that moment at my kitchen table with John Donne), as a single narrative. Not only have I ceased to feel ashamed of my academic storytelling, I have begun to understand the interdependency and the long reach of the stories of which I am part. My novel writing, my grandmother's bookshelf, and my profession as a book historian are all, in fact, part of the same plot. After all, 'English literature' and my grandparents grew up together; just as literature was establishing itself in universities with a select canon of works, my grandparents – for whom university was out of the question – were becoming readers. The books they chose – because of the class they were from – were not going to be the books studied at university. In fact their choices may have been a form of unconscious active resistance. Guilt-free, they read John Buchan and Florence Barclay and consulted *The Wonderland of Knowledge* for compressed tit-bits of history and science. They read the local paper and *The People's Friend*. But their strong class-consciousness – encompassing their proud literacy as well as its mainstream tastes – and their storytelling nudged me into writing popular (not literary) fiction, just as surely as it also initially nudged me away from university, and finally back again. Without these parallel stories, filled with conflict and colour and the politics of exclusion, I would never have been piqued into pursuing my particular specialism, the archaeology of literary taste. In fact, it's not over-stating the case to say that without them I would have no reason to write at all.

The End

I recently told an esteemed colleague and friend that at the Open University we were starting to teach Creative Writing. He was appalled. Why Creative Writing, he demanded? Surely it is just a fad, designed to support less lucrative subjects in our current cash-strapped climate? Why can we not teach Uncreative writing (by which he meant essay technique), since most students have no idea how to string a sentence together, let alone an argument?

He is by no means alone in this opinion; most teachers of Creative Writing have run up against this objection more than once. So exactly what is it they object to? What is the difference between Creative Writing and any other kind of writing? Isn't an essay creative? Well, in my own case, I can answer categorically yes. Thinking of myself as a creative writer might make me a bad literary historian, but I don't think so. In fact I think it makes me a better historian; I am certainly careful not to make stuff up, but I am more alert, perhaps, to the human dramas hidden behind the facts; maybe a little more aware of the ironies and the paradoxes and the contradictions that make up human history.

But what is *Uncreative* writing? A mere listing of the facts? That would be a dull and unhelpful sort of scholarship, and indeed, unacceptable at a professional level. We require intelligent *interpretation* of the facts in order to render them useful, palatable, and persuasive. And the moment we start interpreting – selecting, ordering, arguing with other critics, casting facts in a particular light for a particular purpose – we start creating. Fiction and essay writing are not the same thing, but like it or not, storytelling strategies are everywhere, including universities.

But aren't we just giving people false hope, my colleague demanded? Aren't we just encouraging a rash of mediocre writing and thereby diminishing the quality both of what gets sent to publishers, and of our own degrees? At the Open University, we have found that the opposite is true. We run six ten-credit point 'Start Writing' courses at Level 1, and at the time of writing have just launched a 60-credit point Creative Writing course at Level 2. Not hugely different in structure from courses run in many other institutions, but one of the incidental advantages of a modular system through which students can build their own degree has been that the feedback about different combinations of courses can register surprising results. In this case the feedback suggests that the students are way ahead of the objectors in understanding; those who took 'Start Writing Fiction' have often found it just as useful on other more 'academic' courses as those who took 'Start Writing Essays'. Time and again, student postings on the online conference sites express the enthusiasm of people who have discovered through Creative Writing courses that they can accomplish a range of writing tasks. Contrary to what most critics of University-level Creative Writing assume, these students don't always think that they're going to win the Booker Prize and they don't deluge publishers with bad manuscripts; instead they find they can tackle degree-level essays with greater skill and confidence, and get on and do so.

Creative Writing courses do sometimes turn out wonderful novelists and poets and dramatists. That is our hope, and the hope of many of our students. But far more frequently they turn out students – and later professionals – who have simply learned to write better, and to understand more. Stories have the power, not just to reveal meaning, but also to change it. Storytelling for me enabled, first, a career I had always thought beyond me, and second, a new understanding of my own history. If we let them, stories can transform life for other students too.

9

Documentary Storytelling: The Shaping of Reality

Sarah Boston

Documentaries are constructed not out of the imagination of a fiction writer but out of the raw material of the world about us. The ability to capture that raw material on film was greatly enhanced in the 1960s when lightweight 16mm cameras, with synchronous sound, came into use. The new technology brought about a change in documentary [1] film-making and the stories documentaries could tell. The older static documentaries, overloaded with narration, interpreting the world in voices which patronised the subject and the audience, which had dominated television, were called into question. Instead of a white, male, middle-class voice telling us what Mrs Smith, who worked in a textile factory, thought about her work, Mrs Smith could tell us herself, and what was more we could watch her going to work, working, on her lunch break and even capture her getting on the bus to go home, with a realism and immediacy that had never been caught on camera before. With this new technology came the ability to tell new stories, capturing much more intimately the lives of people, and a whole Pandora's box of questions about the ethics of documentary storytelling was opened.

In documentary storytelling, the late 1960s marked the big divide between 'before and after'. 'Before' was film-making from the earliest days of moving cameras, consisting of a body of work by documentary film-makers, most of which I was then ignorant about and later came to study. 'After' is the body of work, much of it the basis of television documentaries over the past four decades, dominated by observational filming. Modern lighter-weight digital cameras enable even greater intimacy for the film-maker and even cheaper programmes for the broadcaster. To those now with their own digital cameras, be they amateur or professional, it is hard to communicate the excitement and shock of those 1960s documentaries made with the new lightweight equipment.

The first two documentaries I watched of this new genre, called Direct Cinema, were *Warrendale* (1967) and *A Married Couple* (1969), made by the Canadian film-maker, Allan King. In *Warrendale* the camera crew, like 'a fly on the wall', followed for seven weeks the lives of emotionally disturbed children in a treatment centre of the same name. The documentary won the Prix d'art et d'essai at Cannes in 1967 but the Canadian Broadcasting Commission, which had commissioned the film in 1966, refused to air it and it was banned from television for 30 years. Allan King's next documentary, *A Married Couple*, observationally filmed, over a period of time, a couple whose marriage was in trouble. Both films left their audiences, for different reasons, deeply troubled and uncomfortable. Both films raised profound questions about documentary film-makers and their role in telling stories based on real people.

Fiction films and documentaries share many of the same elements of storytelling, but there are two key differences. Documentarists are expected to be telling 'the truth' (a tricky concept) and they have (or should have) a responsibility to their subjects. Both *Warrendale* and *A Married Couple* triggered concern on both fronts. *Warrendale* was made with good intent. Allan King hoped to show how a particular form of care pioneered in Warrendale could and should be followed by others. That care took the form of a grown-up holding a child who was screaming, shouting, kicking, punching until the child was calmed. The 'holding' was to assure the child that he or she was not abandoned. Some of the scenes in the film are deeply disturbing and shocking. The film was intended to bring about positive change in the care of emotionally disturbed children. For Canadian Broadcasting it was thought too raw for a TV audience. I do not know if they questioned whether it was ethical for children, who could not have given informed consent, to be filmed in such a disturbed state. Ethics are an ever-present issue particularly in this style of documentary film-making. [2] Besides the question of the initial consent of a subject there is the ethical question of the legacy on the subjects' lives of their behaviour at that particular moment in their life being shown to the public. After seeing *Warrendale* I felt torn between the public interest defence for its screening and concerns about the private exploitation of its subjects. I had no such mixed feelings after watching *A Married Couple.* To me it was invasive, used its subjects as 'good material' for a dramatic film and played to the voyeuristic appetite of the audience. Such marital disharmony is both ethically, and better, portrayed in fiction – who can forget Richard Burton and Elizabeth Taylor in *Who's Afraid of Virginia Woolf?* I thought Allan King's film indefensible but I remember others arguing that it gave us 'real life – in the raw' and their excitement at the possibilities of filming or watching more 'true life' was tangible. Many current television programmes are the direct descendants of *Warrendale* and *A Married Couple* and the debate around their ethics and their claim to 'truth' continues.

Since that time questions concerning 'The Truth' have dogged documentary film-making. The ideologues of Direct Cinema and their camp followers argue that their non-interventionist, observational style of film-making captures 'the truth' and that all other documentary styles are constructs and thus dishonest. All documentary film-making is a construct and no style has any greater claim on 'the truth' than any other. Despite this there are those who commission documentaries for TV, and the makers of those documentaries, who still maintain that the 'fly-on-the-wall' style is a truthful witness. What is important is that the relationship between the claims the film makes to veracity and the audience, like a contractual relationship, is based on an honesty. If you fake it and don't let your audience know it is fakery then, when you are caught out, the whole story is brought into question. If, audiences, myself included, find out after watching the documentary *The Connection* (Carlton 1996) that we had been lied to (in this case that the drug-runner from Columbia did not swallow and fly with packages of heroin inside him as shown on the film) the edifice of the film comes tumbling down. It falls apart not because, as in fiction, we are bored, it doesn't make sense, the characters or plot are dull, we feel it is not 'true to life', etc. but because we come to watch a documentary with different expectations – an expectation of honest intent. You may disagree with Michael Moore's argument in his films; feel manipulated by his choice of interviewees, situations, comment; you may think he has a super-ego to go with his supersize but his films are not fakes. He sets out his stall and the audience can like it or leave it.

It was in this exciting maelstrom in the late 1960s and the arguments about documentary style, content, ethics and claims to tell 'the truth' that I made my first documentary. It was a 30-minute film for Granada local programmes. The subject, influenced by the Direct Cinema I had seen, was a class of ten-years-olds in a deprived area of Salford a stone's throw from the *Coronation Street* set. I eschewed commentary and used an observational style, but even then I questioned the full purist 'fly-on-the-wall' doctrine. The film set out to capture the world of those ten-year-olds with no planned narrative structure – something I hadn't understood documentaries needed. In the editing a thematic structure was created by using chapter headings in the form of inter-titles. These chapters focused on different aspects of the children's day at school, such as the playground, the school trip, a class, and what they ate – a subject about which I asked the kids. The one re-enacted scene was a poem written by a boy named Billy about his school trip to the Manchester docks. He was a tough little boy. I will never forget his face when he read me his poem. My spontaneous reaction was "Billy, that is wonderful". His face lit up and I asked him to read it for the camera – which he did. That was my first lesson in the responsibility of the film-maker to an individual. I knew I had to keep the poem in the film or, if I didn't use it, the small boost I had given to Billy's self-esteem would be shattered. It is in the film. The playground sequence was cut to the Rolling Stone's number 'Street Fighting Man' – my first attempt at a montage created out of sounds, words and images. Although I had a strong idea of the film I wanted to make, I knew almost nothing about the technology and grammar of film or directing. I had a professional camera crew and a film editor who brought great skill and creativity to the story I wanted to tell. Without their skills the whole project would have been a disaster. Granada broadcast my film entitled, '*Til We Have Built Jerusalem*, and it was only later, after I had left Granada, I learnt that following its transmission Salford Education Authority was so appalled at what had been portrayed that they banned, for quite some time, any other film-makers from filming in their schools. This was to be my first and last observational film but not because it displeased Salford Education Authority.

I left Granada as they had made me an offer I had to refuse and it was some time before I got my next break. I used my time, and dole money, between these two experiences of film-making to start myself on a course of study about documentary, both technical and its history. The technical education came about through joining a women's group called 'The London Women's Film Group' and one of the group's aims was to empower ourselves by learning how to use a 16mm camera and to light, record sound and edit. It was an invaluable experience if only to make me realise that I was, in the practical sense, technically challenged. But the basic understanding of the grammar of film gained from doing all the jobs in the process of film-making has stood me in good stead ever since. Although the technologies have changed I regularly say to my students: "whatever the technology, it is still about storytelling – the technology is only a means to an end."

My journey of discovery of the history of documentary film-making – the films that had been made and what the film-makers had written and thought about the form – was the really important discovery of that period of my life. My education was random due to the fact I had to wait for a documentary to be shown at the NFT or turn up at some film club. It was with stunned amazement I watched Dziga Vertov's *A Man With A Movie Camera* (1929). Vertov's filmic manifestation of his theory, Kino Pravda (Film Truth), is the absolute opposite filmic form to Direct Cinema.

In it, Vertov, with great energy, excitement and humour, films the streets, people and cars of a city. A cameraman and his camera are a character in the film so that the process of film, far from being invisible, are reflectively visible. The editing, a fast montage, was, and is, quite spectacular. Vertov's montage led me to read Sergei Eisenstein and his theories of editing.[3] Opened up to me was a whole new dynamic of storytelling. Image could be cut against image in dialectical ways, liberating the film-maker from telling a story in a linear way. This led me back to Bertolt Brecht, whom I had studied at university, and his assertion "art is not a mirror held up to reality, but a hammer with which to shape it." [4] John Grierson, the father of the British documentary tradition, now sadly largely forgotten, described this process as the "creative treatment of actuality" and the word "creative" should be stressed. [5] As a result I rejected the Direct Cinema 'mirror' approach to documentary film-making. Being a 'fly-on-the-wall' excluded the possibility of finding out what people think, of putting personal stories within a social, historical and economic context, and the infinite choices the dynamic of film allows. Later, to add to that dynamic, came sound and all the possibilities of combining sound and image.

To give a crude example of the possibilities of sound and image, had the above paragraph been part of a sync interview for a biographical film about me, its usages in a documentary could be many. The formulaic way, employed endlessly by the Biography Channel, would be to literally illustrate, where possible, what I said. So there would be me walking into the NFT, a clip of *A Man With a Movie Camera*, me sitting reading Sergei Eisenstein, a shot of the University of Sussex English Department and, more problematical, me transmogrified into a fly. Or the layering of my voice over inter-cutting clips from Vertov and what were then (early 1970s) TV factual programmes, would add a more interesting illustrative visual dimension to what I am saying. You could do a reverse shot or two of a camera crew filming me, both echoing Vertov and reminding the audience that documentary is a construct. A third way could be edited so that you see images of me directing a 'fly-on-the-wall' film while hearing me talk about my rejection of that style, the visual imagery working in direct contradiction to what is being said. The first approach is storytelling with pictures – an illustrated book. The second visually signals the content and adds a layering of meaning. And the third option would be the film-maker implying that although I (the subject) intellectually rejected being a 'fly-on-the-wall' I had, for whatever ever reason, sold out. It is this layering of meaning that film allows which I call non-linear storytelling.

My journey of discovery opened up other styles of film-making, in particular, images and the power of imagery in the telling of documentary stories. These documentaries, described as poetic, were pioneered by film-makers such as Joris Ivens and Walter Ruttman in the 1920s and 1930s. Ivens in *Rain* (1929) told, through images and sounds, the story of a shower of rain passing over Amsterdam and with the same impressionistic style Walter Ruttman celebrated a city, in *Berlin, Symphony of a City* (1927). Both these films and others that followed in the 'poetic' genre share a way of storytelling that is non-linear. Continuity editing is sacrificed for sequences of images that may have no temporal or spatial relationship. Sounds are used creatively and voices sparingly. The British master of the poetic documentary was Humphrey Jennings. *Listen To Britain* (1942) and *Diary For Timothy* (1945) left a deep impression on me and in particular how a story could so poetically be communicated through sound and image. Most powerful of all poetic films, and it has lost none of its power is, Alain Renais' *Night and Fog* (1955). Leni Riefenstahl's film about the Nuremberg Rally, *The Triumph of the Will* (1937), is a lesson in the power of imagery and its dangers.

In this journey of discovery (one which I continue) I was looking to find ways in which I could tell the stories; ways that could be richer, more complex and engaging emotionally and intellectually than that which purely observational film-making could achieve. I learnt from watching this range of films that the style chosen dictates the parameters of the narrative structure. Choosing a style is like a self-denying ordinance, as with creative writing, for stylistic integrity has to be maintained but within that artistic constraint there are many choices. After my first documentary I looked, with each film, to find a form that best suited the content and rejected trying to shoehorn all stories into one style. Each story presents new problems in its telling and trying to find a way that tells that story in its most engaging form is always a challenge.

What I also learnt intellectually watching those films, and then learnt through the making of more than thirty documentaries, was that narrative structure, as with fiction, underlies all good stories. Rarely does the content and form for a documentary come in one flash of inspiration. One of the few occasions it did for me was, when the final credits rolled over a documentary about Woody Guthrie, and I thought, "It would be great to make a film marking the 50th anniversary of John Steinbeck's novel, *The Grapes of Wrath*, and retrace the journey of the Joad family portrayed in the novel from eastern Oklahoma to California interweaving the past and present." That basic underlying structure never changed though it became much more multi-layered in its making and editing.

Usually one begins with an idea or a subject but one is at a loss as to how to turn that idea into a story. It is in the process of research, of talking to people, discussing the idea with others and of looking and listening, that a way of telling a story emerges. From my experience, and that of my colleagues, this is the stage that many students, like professionals, struggle with. The problem with students is that they often don't understand that before setting out to film you need to have a story to tell. They have a subject, an issue, an idea that they think would make a great documentary and when you ask them, "How are you going to tell the story?", they look hurt and say, defending their idea, "Oh well, I'll interview some people and well, um, film, um, you know ..." Or, the technocrats answer by saying how they are going to "use split screen and HD and fish-eye lenses to ... and um ..." and then they trail off into mumbling.

Starting out on a shoot with a clear idea of what one wants is not only immensely time-saving (and time is money when filming) but it is much more likely to ensure that the raw material gained is what is needed to make the film. I am often asked who writes my scripts. Sometimes I reply facetiously, "life", but a serious explanation is that I work from a structure. I set out on a film having worked out the main ingredients that I need with which to tell the story. This structure forms the schedule and schedules are based on time and money. It is a balancing act between not being able to get all you want but ensuring you get what you need. For documentarists who are not working to a script one of the problems when filming is that it is easy to be distracted by other interesting stories than the one you set out to tell. The camera person will see shots, great though they may be, but which you know have no relevance to the story. Scenes unfold before your eyes and, unless you are focused on the story you are telling, you have no way of deciding whether to film them or not. In interviewing people you may well use up hours of time and tape getting some riveting life story when you know you only want a contribution relevant to the film. Fortunately, trained on 16mm film, which made one aware that money was going through the gate every time the camera was rolling, you had to learn to be very focused on the story you were telling, a focus forged in the pre-production stage. Unfortunately now it is so cheap to turn on a camera that the importance of finding that focus in pre-production is seen as having much less importance.

The editing stage is the creative core of documentary film-making. It is in the post-production process that the narrative structure is hammered out. My way, and it has never changed, is to sit at my kitchen table with a log of everything shot, the transcripts of everything said in the film, and out of that I construct my paper edit. This process involves cutting out bits of the transcripts, sticking them down, adding in for the editor indications of visual material that may work with that section, and then sitting back and reading it like a story. At times my kitchen table is covered with bits of paper accepted or rejected, stuck down, moved, re-stuck as I try to get the story straight. That paper edit forms the first rough assembly of the film. The first viewing immediately reveals the flaws in the paper-edit, and until the backbone narrative structure is achieved you cannot move forward to the finer tuning of the film. In that finer tuning you are not just smoothing out bad cuts but you are building into the film its rhythm and pace. You are sensing when the film should move fast or be slowed down; when a pause is needed or the pause is too long. It is in the editing that the dynamic of film comes to life. Meaning can be enhanced, stressed or changed in the combination of sound and images that are chosen.

Documentaries have been told in a variety of rich and complex styles for over a century. You only have to go to one of the international documentary film festivals to be reassured that independent film-makers continue to be challenged and challenging in the shaping of reality. Sadly the ratings race of television in the UK today has almost completely closed down TV openings for documentarists who wish to explore actuality in such ways. My luck was that, even though getting commissions always seemed a long, hard struggle, much of my documentary career coincided with the opening up of television to serious documentaries. In the mid-1960s BBC2 came on line – a whole new channel with slots for documentaries and one that was not in direct competition with ITV for ratings; ITV itself was in those days quite heavily regulated and required to provide a percentage of serious factual programmes; and then in 1982 Channel

4 began broadcasting with a remit to "foster the new and experimental in television" and to "develop ideas for which the existing services have not so far found a place". A remit its first controller, Jeremy Isaacs, took seriously. [6] This openness enabled me to make programmes exploring the dynamic of film and all I had learnt about it.

Working for an independent company of which I was/am a part (as opposed to as a freelancer temporarily working in-house for the BBC or ITV) has enabled me since the 1980s to make films that I and my colleagues feel ethically at ease with. The problem of responsibility to the people who are in my films, which so troubled me at the outset of my career, was solved by working *with* people – telling stories they wanted to tell and I thought should be heard – rather than me telling stories *about* them. I have never had a problem with allowing interviewees to see a fine cut of a film (which the BBC views as an unacceptable practice) and changing anything they wish changed. Many documentarists believe to work in such a way would mean that they would lose power and control. For me it has been a way of working that has enhanced the stories I have been able to tell, and I have never felt it an artistic constraint. 'The Truth' (with one dramatic exception in which I, the producer, the production team and the commissioning editor at Channel 4 'fell for' a story that was untrue) has not been an issue that has much troubled me. That sounds as though I have some cavalier disdain for its importance. I set out in my documentaries to tell a story with no claims to objectivity or to asserting the film has some purchase on 'the truth'. The style sets out my stall. It is my 'creative interpretation' hammered out of actuality by all the skills and creativity of everyone that has contributed to its making.

Notes

[1] I use the term 'documentary' to refer mainly to the single documentary and a few documentary series, not docu-soaps, formatted documentary series and factual entertainment or current affairs programmes, which are, in the UK, made under certain regulatory strictures not applied to documentaries.

[2] Bill Nichols, *Introduction to Documentary*, (Bloomington: Indiana University Press, 2001). (See Chapter 1, 'Why Are Ethical Issues Central to Documentary Filmmaking?').

[3] Sergei Eisenstein, *Film Form: Essays in Film Theory*, trans. Jay Leyda, (Dennis Dobson, 1963), Michael Glenny and Richard Taylor, eds., *Eisenstein Vol. 2 Towards a Theory of Montage*, trans. Michael Glenny, (BFI Publishing, 1991).

[4] This statement is generally attributed to Bertolt Brecht. However, some attribute the saying to the Russian writer, Vladimir Mayakovsky, others believe it was Karl Marx, and even Leon Trotsky has been given the credit.

[5] John Grierson, *Grierson on Documentary*, (Faber, 1966).

[6] Stephen Lambert, *Channel Four*, (BFI Publishing, 1982).

10

Calling Time

Michelene Wandor

Check the time on your watch.

> Modern Western commonsense organises time into a linear
> chronology of hours, days, years, within a structure of shared
> fantasy. This is held in place by the movement of the sun,
> together with a mythical but altogether effective anchoring
> point, the year of the birth of Jesus (other cultures manage
> just as efficiently with a different regulatory date-line) ... If
> you believe in it, it works. [1]

We take time for granted, until, that is, we travel to another country,
in another time zone. Our bodies have been chugging along in their
own time, and then, within five to six hours, we might be in New
York. Our bodies think we are five to six hours older but, hey presto,
the time of day tells us we are five to six hours younger. Theoretically,
then, if you travel round the world backwards, you could solve the
problem of ageing. But I am beginning to indulge in flights of fancy
(the only kind of flight which is good for the ozone layer). Time is
all about pragmatic conceptualisation. Time was only standardised
in the UK with the arrival of the railways in the early 19th century.

This essay is about some ways of thinking about time in relation
to writing.

We are constructed by time. Culturally as well as biologically.

Time motors us. Time is intangible, non-material and yet it is – literally – the regulatory mechanism which orders the structure of our lives, and the shape of our work and relationships. We talk about 'body clocks'; some people are always late, some people are always early. Playing music entails 'keeping time', as if it is something which has to be contained, nurtured and retained. Unless the ensemble is operating with exactly the same rhythm and timing, the music falls apart.

I know someone who doesn't wear a watch. He says he has plenty of time. It's all around him.

> There is lived time.
> There is reading time.
> There is writing time.
> They may correspond.
> They may not.
> They cannot.

The time it takes to write something is longer than the time it takes to read something.

The time it takes to think something is shorter than the time it takes to write something.

> The time it takes!
> Time takes time.

The end of Caryl Churchill's play, *Top Girls*, takes two forms: on the page and on the stage. The stage directions before the last scene in print say that it actually takes place a year before the penultimate scene – if you follow me. Anyone reading the play in book form will automatically flip a mental time-switch and imagine/read the scene as a 'flashback', a common novelistic device. However, when you see the play on the stage, you simply see the last scene in what appears to be a chronological sequence, so that it takes place (in theatrical time) *after* the penultimate scene, as you would expect. There is nothing (i.e., no particular event, no significant clue in the words exchanged) in the final scene you see (which has actually already taken place a year earlier) which would enable the audience to 'know' that – etc., etc.

Time in the theatre is a far simpler beast than it is in the novel. Apparently. Time in the theatre is mostly divided between the exciting contradiction between the clock-based chronology of performance time (the play begins at 7.30pm, and ticks its way through the 24-hour watch on your wrist, until 10.00pm), and the theatrical imperatives of the historic time within the fictional world of the play, which can be anything, from the Aristotelian unity of time (i.e., the play takes place in a historical time which corresponds exactly to the performance time), to 5,000 years or three weeks or seven months. If it is, for example, *Hamlet*, we know that it was written at the end of the 16th, beginning of the 17th century, we know that it is set somewhere back in the middle ages, when the story of Hamnett took historic place; within the play itself, the action moves forward in time, and also ventures into supernatural time, when the ghost comes and goes.

Each scene lasts a certain amount of time, sometimes as close to 'real' theatrical time as it takes to perform the scene's actions; between each scene, a certain amount of time elapses. Sometimes this is clear, sometimes it is variable. Sometimes it matters. Mostly, it tends not to matter. We assume time has passed, without concerning ourselves about whether it is two hours, or overnight or three weeks. We assume that the order in which we see scenes on a stage is also the order in which the events happen – unless there is some device (a caption, for example) which signals a significant movement in time, forwards or backwards.

The deployment of time in the novel works differently. I have just finished reading a novel in which each section is headed with a date. Not only does the story range between 1858 and 2003, there is also a section towards the end where it alternates backwards and forwards between present and past. In a sense, because my reading follows the numbering of the pages, I am reading on the assumption that the action moves forward. If I want to read it in the historical date-order in which the events 'happened', I would have to make a list of dates, and flip around in the book in order to read them in that order.

So a curious thing is happening: as I read my way *forward* through the book, moving *forward* in my own (!) time (i.e., I started reading the book at 6pm on Monday and finished it at 2pm on Tuesday – I read fast), I was absorbing the story *as if* one event followed the next in chronological time just as it was arranged on the book's pages, and as I was reading it; at the same time I *knew* (because the dates told me) that I was actually reading *backwards*, in a sense, and engaging in an oddly impossible activity. I was reading events in non-chronological order, and 'reading' events in chronological order at another cognitive, imaginative level. I hope I have got the logic of that right, and I hope you are still with me. I hope you have also noted the changes of tense in this paragraph.

> … to narrate a story is already to "reflect upon" the event narrated. [2]

> … the time taken to narrate and the time of the things narrated.[3]

Verb tenses are obvious indicators – present, past, and occasionally future. The choice of tenses is, of course, crucial. A shift between different points of view in a narrative can also entail a movement back in time, as well as a change in perspective on the events in that time.

Check the time on your watch.
How long did it take to read this chapter?
Did you read it all at once?
How long did it take me to write it?
Not telling.
I don't know.
I didn't add up all the bits of time I spent at the computer.
I didn't distil and add up all the bits of time I spent taking notes from various books.
I didn't add up the time I spent thinking about bits of the chapter.
I didn't add up the time spent exchanging emails with Maggie Butt, apologising for being late with the chapter, then telling her it was on its way.

It should read all of a piece; as if its internal logic(s) give(s) the strong impression that it all flowed together, at a single sitting. Why?

Your time spent reading this is more computable than my time spent thinking and administering and writing this.

> ... the perfect tense is the present in the past and the future is the present to come. [4]

Check your watch.

> Modern Western commonsense organised time into a linear chronology of hours, days, years, within a structure of shared fantasy. This was held in place by the movement of the sun, together with a mythical but altogether effective anchoring point, the year of the birth of Jesus (other cultures managed just as efficiently with a different regulatory date-line) ... If you believed in it, it worked. [5]

This is now science fiction, describing a world in which people had a very strange concept of time, controlled by the movement of the sun and the earth in relation to one another. In this new science fiction world, of course, we know that time and space are a continuum, and we tell space just as in the olden days they used to tell time. Notice that my use of the present tense here is an illusion. It is actually a tense which refers to a future time, which I am imagining I am actually living, and that is why it is in the present tense. By the time you read this, the moment of writing, when I feel the present tense as the tense of the writing, will be past. Your reading of it will be in your present moment of time, which will appear as if it corresponds to mine, thus giving the illusion that we are actually communicating. Be disabused. We are not. You are no more my audience than I am addressing you.

These are only some of the illusions with which we play in written language. Do not believe any of them, not once or many times.

Now. Here's an interesting thing to do.

Take a short story of your own. Or take a short story written by someone else. It doesn't matter what it is, whether it is good, bad or indifferent, whether it is written by someone famous or not.

Read the story.

Re-read the story.

Note down how much fictional time elapses between the very

beginning and the very end.

Then take a single page of the story (it doesn't matter which one). Type it out, double-spaced.

Then mark in the margin(s) the *gaps* in time within the narrative itself. There will always be time gaps, because all narrative narrates within a time span of some kind.

First mark where the gaps occur.

Then mark how long elapses in each time gap.

Sometimes it will be clear, sometimes it won't.

Leave the page, and return to it a week later.

Re-read it, and see if there are any more time markings to be added.

It's time to go.

Check your watch.

What's the time?

Notes

[1] Anthony Easthope, *Privileging Difference* (Palgrave, 2002), p.7.

[2] Paul Ricoeur, translated by Kathleen McLaughlin and David Pellauer, *Time and Narrative*, Vol. 2, (University of Chicago Press, 1985), p.61.

[3] Ibid., p.100.

[4] Ibid., p.64.

[5] Anthony Easthope, *Privileging Difference* (Palgrave, 2002), p.7. But this is re-written, so it is not, strictly speaking, Anthony Easthope's 'as originally written' quote.

11

Just Whose Journey is This?
A Radical Approach to the Question of
the 'Journey' Taken in Scripts

James Martin Charlton

When those involved in the Scriptwriting process – whether for stage or screen – talk about what goes on in scripts, we hear a lot about 'journeys'. The story is referred to as a journey, the characters are expected to go on a journey, and one American writer has even written a whole volume describing scripts as "The Writer's Journey", a kind of Shamanistic descent into Archetypes and Mythic Structures in which the writer dives for mythic gold [1]. My feeling is that such discussions and points of view miss out on mentioning the one really important journey which goes on as any narrative unfolds – the journey of the audience member. The drama actually takes place in a couple (give or take) of hours of the audience member's life, and the role of the writer is to take them on a journey for that time. The journey of the characters is but a medium facilitating the audience's journey. The writer's own journey – well, who is interested except his or her own family and friends? In what follows, I shall deal with the idea of taking the audience on a journey with specific reference to the thinking and planning which has gone into some of the tours I have offered audiences of my own plays.

I am a radical dramatist, just as Ibsen, Shaw, Jean Genet or Edward Bond were/are radical. My purpose is to create scripts which are not 'a night *out*' from the audience's life rather but an event which takes place *in* the life of the audience member. I do not take the view that you switch off history – personal or social – when you step inside a theatre or cinema. These are not *sacred spaces* set aside as a refuge or an escape. They are places within our specific historical and social circumstance, staffed and manned by people who must earn wages to survive in a particular economic reality, and the events which unfold in the plays and films which are shown in these spaces will have an effect upon that reality one way or another. The effect will either be conservative – they will uphold and confirm certain social circumstances – or radical – in that they will challenge or even undermine the social circumstances in which the theatre or cinema exists. One could say that, therefore, a film or play needs to be 'about' the world outside the theatre or cinema. Yet the social world 'outside' is not 'outside' at all – the social world is in the theatre and cinema in just the same way as it is everywhere else. In his book *The Hidden Plot*, Edward Bond asks "is theatre about life or *of* life" and comes to the conclusion that "as there is no discontinuity between the two stages" – the 'world stage' and the 'theatre stage' – therefore "drama is not merely about life but is *of* life. Nor may we ever escape from the stage – as we may escape from our clothes by undressing." [2] We are the same people when we watch a play or a film as when we have our tickets torn by the usher or we do the tasks which earn us our wages or we interact with our lovers or we take care of our children. Therefore, me writing a script is me having other human beings *in my clutches* for a period of time. I am going to do something with them, in exactly the same way as I might exchange a smile or argue with an usher, like or dislike those I work with or for, pleasure or challenge a lover, teach or play with a child.

I said above that films or plays can be either conservative or radical. To see an example of a conservative script, one only has to look at any of the many police dramas or crime stories which fill up our TV screens on a nightly basis. The basic plot is generally the same – a crime of violence (usually a murder) is committed and someone – a representative of the state or an enthusiastic amateur acting in the interests of the state – solves the crime and takes away the freedom of the criminal, either by arresting the person themselves (in the case of the professional law keeper) or handing the miscreant over to the state (in the case of the amateur sleuth). This simple plot is a genre stereotype, and most crime drama plays out along these lines. The journey of the characters is either one of *solving* or *being solved*. The journey of the audience is one of *reassurance*. The events of the story intervene in the audience's life in order to tell him or her that crime does not pay, that the state is looking after us – or if the state is neglectful or incompetent, a socially-minded individual will do the job – and that we live in a word ruled by justice. We can – literally – sleep easily in our beds, knowing that order asserts itself against the forces of chaos and the transgressors of our social order (the social order is usually seen as a cohesive whole in popular crime drama). The drama has an actual, narcotic effect on the viewer, as real as any sleeping pill or potion. The act of being taken through the events of a crime story – of being horrified (perhaps excited?) by the crime, of worrying along with the victims and crime busters, of feeling the satisfaction of justice being seen to be done – is part and parcel of an action which includes sitting on the sofa with a cup of tea at the outset of the programme and getting up and feeding the cat at the close. You have done something with someone whilst sitting on that sofa; someone has done something with you.

It is, of course, possible for writers and other makers of drama to bend a conservative genre to their own ends, to take part in an act of *subversion*. In Roman Polanski's 1974 film *Chinatown*, all of the elements of the classic film noir are present and we expect the events of the story – peopled as it is with shady characters and *femme fatales* – to take us to the usual hard-bitten conclusions of the genre: that women are devils and bad guys get what's coming to them. The film leads its audience down a well-trodden garden path only to leave them at an unusual finale. The woman in the film is not a *femme fatale* after all – everything she has done has been through good intentions – and the villain wins the day with a shocking and absolute finality. The effect is both destabilising and depressing. We have been confronted by the fact that a corrupt and Patriarchal order owns everything – from the police department to the very water we drink – and gets away with anything – from murder to incest and child abuse. The honest man doesn't have a hope in hell of sorting this out, and the audience is left with the final words spoken to the protagonist in the film – "forget it Jake, it's Chinatown."[3] We are left with the same choice as the character – do we forget what we have seen – the corruption and the abuse of power – or do we attempt to raise ourselves to action against these things? We can, along with Jake, either forget *Chinatown* (it is 'just a film' after all) or we can allow it to haunt us, as it will surely haunt Jake. Whether the approach taken by the scriptwriter and director is an encouraging or discouraging one – whether it is likely to have an energising effect or one of resignation on the viewer – is debatable. Certainly Murray Sperber has argued that the 'message' of the film is "do as little as possible" and that the filmmaker Polanski is "smiling at the folks out there, assuming that he has gotten us to accept his vision of corruption and nihilism." [4] What is unarguable is that *Chinatown* is an experience within life which will have an effect in the lives of its audiences.

In the case of *Chinatown*, it is difficult to tell whether Polanski and the scriptwriter, Robert Towne, are definitively radical or conservative. The script departs from genre stereotypes, a radical act, at the same time as possibly encouraging inertia, an act of deep conservatism. Its lack of reassuring news could be seen as, in itself, assuring us, like Beckett's tramps, that there is "Nothing to be done". [5] The options open to the radical dramatist often fall within two parameters – to subvert an existing genre with the unexpected or unusual, or to depart from genre or conventional forms of storytelling altogether. Before I go on to discuss some of my own methods, I will examine two examples of radical dramaturgy, one *subversive*, the other *innovative*.

Henrik Ibsen's 1879 play, *A Doll's House*, is a subversive work which operates in a specific genre whilst at the same time confounding genre expectations for a radical purpose. Ibsen's drama operates within the tradition of 'the Well-Made Play' – a genre of theatre from the 19th century which involves a very tight plot with a climax that takes place close to the end of the story, in which most of the actual story takes place before the play's action; information about such previous action is revealed through thinly veiled exposition, followed by a series of causally related plot complications. Often, the drama uses the device of letters or papers falling into unintended hands in order to bring about plot twists and climaxes. One glance at the play itself will reveal its close adherence to these dramatic conventions. However, the Well-Made Play was expected to end with the restoration of order, whereas in *A Doll's House* the protagonist, Nora, refuses to return to normality after her marriage has been exposed as a sham based not on love but social custom. This ending proved too much for many in the play's original audience to take. They were happy to be taken on a journey which involved the shaking of certain foundations, as long as the house (a fine bourgeois property) remained standing, strong as ever, at the play's close. That the house in Ibsen's play was (figuratively) destroyed, scared the audience, because they knew on some level that what was happening on stage was intimately connected to the world off stage, and the sight of a woman walking out of a marriage on stage might encourage women to walk out of their marriages off stage. So it came to pass, and the enormous changes in women's place in society, her marital expectations and economic independence, which have taken place in the West in the century or so since Ibsen's play was first written and performed were almost certainly helped on their way by *A Doll's House*.

A more radical approach to dramaturgy – hardly based in dramatic conventions at all – is taken by Edward Bond in his notorious 1965 play *Saved*. The play is set in a working-class area of south London. It tells the story of a single mother's on-off relationships with a couple of men in her life. In Scene Six of the play, the supposed father of her child and a gang of his mates stone the baby to death in a park – it is a disturbing and nauseating scene. Conventionally, what an audience might expect to happen is that the crime is investigated and justice is seen to be done. However, although the supposed father does spend a short time in prison, the crime is never 'paid' for; rather, it is portrayed as being a part of the texture of the culturally derelict lives these characters live.

This is dramatically deeply unsatisfying to most audiences, and moreover deeply unsatisfying to any reasonable person's sense of justice. We are a million miles away from the reassurance offered by television crime serials – order has not been re-established and we can't sleep safe in our beds. To illustrate how utterly disorientating Bond's dramaturgy in *Saved* is, we only have to look at Christopher Booker's comments about the play in his book *The Seven Basic Plots*: "Nothing, archetypally, was more chilling in Bond's play than the fact that, after the baby's murder, portrayed in such obsessional detail, so little interest is shown in what happens to its perpetrators, apart from their perfunctory prison sentence." [6] Booker sounds genuinely appalled that Bond should depart so fully and radically from the supposed 'archetypal' rules of narrative structure – pay-offs and pay-backs – and his comments on *Saved* end: "Truly, in this landmark in the history of story-telling, was the dark inversion complete." [7] What Booker means is that his own moral, social and political assumptions have been inverted, his own belief in some innate human ability to create a Universal Order out of chaos has been challenged, his own expectations as a member of the audience have been confounded.

Booker's *The Seven Basic Plots* is an intensely conservative work. It is a book the size and weight and *purpose* of which remind me of the great stone laid against the Sepulchre of Jesus Christ in the Gospel[8]. In a way, it is the storytelling equivalent of a law book – it works by example of precedent. Moreover, Booker buys into the notion of universal humanity which Barthes identified in his *Mythologies*: "It postulates that a universal exists" [9], that "there is one single human nature." [10] For Booker, that Universal and Eternal human nature spins the same stories again and again through time, a notion which is a kind of generalised truth [11] but which rather misses the fact that different times and different societies might need different kinds of stories. Bond's *Saved* was written after two world wars, the holocaust and the atomic bombs at Hiroshima and Nagasaki, and during the Cold War, which in 1963 had brought the world to the brink of nuclear destruction during the Cuban Missile Crisis.

For Bond, such radically challenging times call for radically challenging dramatic techniques. The ways of the past must give way to new methods and new strategies. As Bond says in *The Hidden Plot*:

> The writer must create the *observed*. The writer arrives at this by comparing what has been written and recorded of the past with the maelstrom of the present. You are part of the maelstrom but guided by the past. The past is the shore – and for dramatists that is Chekhov, Ibsen, Strindberg, Brecht. A modern writer needs those writers and many more … *But they are not in the maelstrom with you.* There has to be a new beginning. [12] [Bond's italics.]

I began writing plays in the mid-1980s, during the long years of Thatcherite government, at the outset of the AIDS crisis, hot on the heels of the Falklands War and the miners strike, myself already a veteran of Stop the City demonstrations, Pride marches and punk performance groups. I came to the theatre clutching copies of plays by Edward Bond, Howard Brenton and Joe Orton and with the sound of anarcho-punk resounding in my ears. My very early plays were highly derivative of my influences – ribald Ortonesque farces and violent political cartoons. By the end of the decade, I had managed to write one play – *The World & His Wife* – which I could truly call my own. I had begun to develop *dramatic strategies* of my own.

The narrative of *The World & His Wife* is circular in structure, as befits a play the epigram to which is a quote from Northrop Frye about the cyclical nature of Revolution – "The word 'revolution' itself contains a tragic irony: it is itself a part of the revolving of life and death in a circle of pain." [13] The play begins by introducing an unhappily married couple – Mike and Christine Mann – and plunges the audience head first into a marital barney full of violent and bitter recriminations. Mike hates his wife, feels trapped in the marriage, threatens Christine and rubs in her face that he no longer loves her. However, he will stay with her as she offers him an economic and maternal comfort blanket. In succession, Christine is visited by three callers – a closeted gay vicar addicted to toilet sex, a police detective searching for a serial killer and a militant lesbian feminist who happens to be an old school friend of Christine's. By the time the last appears on the scene, Christine is ripe for a change, and the first act ends with Christine and her by-now lesbian lover unceremoniously and violently ejecting Mike from the house.

Having moved the plot forwards in a fairly traditional way but being aware that the revolutionary event at the end of the first act was not a permanent solution to the problems of the play, I structured the second act as a reverse mirror of the first. Christine is now ensconced with a female partner, and is visited by the vicar who has now 'come out' in a big way, the detective who has caught his man, and finally Mike, trying to inveigle his way back into his old home. This reversal of Act 1 is topped by a set-piece – a 'reverse marriage ceremony' – in which the vicar un-marries the bride and groom and the groom is castrated by the militant lesbian. [14] A coda fast forwards the action by five years, only to show that the relationship between Christine and her woman has deteriorated into the same round of recrimination and bitterness we saw within the heterosexual partnership at the outset of Act 1.

The circular structure of the play takes the audience on a journey of frustration. The actions taken by the characters do not sort out their problems; rather, they tend to more deeply entrench the characters in problematic situations. The audience is offered no assurance that revolution will do anything other than revolve us around to the starting place, as Sisyphus' rock rolled back down the hill each time he made it to the top. This structure was meant to provoke unease in an audience who were the survivors or inheritors of the social and sexual revolutions of the 1960s and who now inhabited a decade in which the surface may have changed but frustration remained as strong as ever. The play was purposefully – as opposed to any bourgeois notion of a good and satisfying night out – a deeply *unsatisfying* experience. Rather than take a person out of his or her self, it was designed to continually turn them back to the historical and personal position they inhabited as they sat down in their theatre seat at the outset. The only difference at the close being that they have *seen the play*. According to Jean-Paul Sartre:

> If society sees itself and, in particular, sees itself as *seen*, there is, by virtue of this very fact, a contesting of the established values of the régime. The writer presents it with its image; he calls upon it to assume it or to change itself. At any rate, it changes; it loses the equilibrium which its ignorance had given it ...[15]

For the radical playwright, this strategy might backfire and create the kind of world-weary lethargy which Sperber accuses *Chinatown* of propagating. To counter this, I made the events the audience encounters in the play as exuberantly violent and obscene as possible. This was the age of the video nasty [16], and watching these as well as a number of popular non-fiction accounts of serial killers, egged me on to depths of offence designed to shake audiences out of any viewer complacency. [17] There are scenes in *The World & His Wife* which literally dare the audience to stay and watch or walk out in outrage and disgust. The stakes involved in the contents of the play are high enough that the audience are forced to make a moral decision as to whether they wish to continue watching the play or not. [18] It also dares them to laugh out loud at the sheer mean-spiritedness and low-down nastiness of these moments. [19]

After a few more plays offering an exuberant and extreme mirror of the ills of our society, I came out of the 1980s looking for solutions and alternatives to those ills. The 1980s had created a selfish and acquisitive society but voices were speaking out against this and some people were trying to develop alternative ways of being. I dramatised this in my play *Fat Souls*, first performed in 1993. The play tells the story of a social misfit and long-time jobseeker, Fat Mags, who gets dead-end employment doing routine dogsbody work in an office. Her fellow workers are mostly concerned with boosting their own fragile egos and status at the expense of others. Mags comes in for a fair bit of abuse, due to her size and social ineptitude. She is befriended by a fellow employee, a simple youth called Lamb, who helps her towards self-respect and an enjoyment of life. When Lamb is murdered by another member of staff, in one of those senseless and brutal attacks one reads about all too often in the newspapers, Mags is tempted to huddle back into the ball of weakness in which she began the play. Lamb appears to her, and this vision of her dead friend gives Mags the strength to continue in her attempt to live a *human* life.

There are two dramatic strategies to be discussed here. One is the return of Lamb from the dead, which (given his name and symbolic resurrection) has a certain Christian resonance. This is, in itself, surprising in a play which is at times brutal and repulsive. I did not utilize this Christian archetype to make any claims to Christian Revelation beyond the play but rather to take the audience on a journey through violence and death and so communicate that this death does not have to be the end of the human connections we make with each other, which is a claim I do make beyond the play. The human moments *live on*. Bob Dylan writes in his song 'In The Summertime': " ... I'm still carrying the gift you gave,/It's a part of me now, it's been cherished and saved." [20] There is an affinity between the unfolding of a play and the unfolding of a recorded album – both enter the mind of the audience/listener and communicate ideas and emotions in the moment, directly into the psyche.

Secondly, although the play is protagonist-driven – it is primarily the story of Fat Mags – the narrative keeps switching focus so that we glimpse the worlds and minds of the other characters, in scenes of dramatic interaction and self-revelatory soliloquies. This is part and parcel of the play's challenge to a bourgeois notion of individuality and selfishness. It may be one person's story but it is all of these other people's stories too. I very much distrust the Hollywood tendency towards scripts centred on the 'journey' or 'growth' of a single individual, especially when that individual is portrayed as the 'rooting interest' – the character the audience is supposed to *identify with* and *root for*. The audience may well identify with Fat Mags and will root for her at times – but I am careful to give every one of her antagonists and tormentors their own human moments, by which the audience are encouraged to empathise with them. In this way, audience assumptions of a clear moral delineation in the dramatis personae, the tendency to reject 'bad' or 'nasty' characters out of hand – to *dehumanise* them – is inhibited. And just perhaps this tendency might be checked in terms of their own 'enemies' in their intrapersonal lives.

Both *The World & His Wife* and *Fat Souls* were dramatic responses to the times in which they were written. Times move on, and my dramatic strategies shift and change. My first feature-length screenplay *Take Me In* (2006), takes the audience on the journey of two naïfs from the sticks who come to London and become house-servants to a wealthy brother and sister. For the most part, the script is an intrapersonal story, along the lines of French Art House cinema like *Un Coeur en hiver* (1992) or *J'embrasse pas* (1991), full of smouldering, underplayed intensity and sly class observation. However, towards the end the events turn dark and an act of unimaginable violence takes place, all the more shocking by being a seeming *non sequitur* given what's gone before. Yet this is the journey on which I wish to take my audience. I mean to lull them into a false sense of security. I let them think they know where they are, what kind of thing this is. Then I plunge them into a world of horror, something out of myth, or more realistically out of Abu Ghraib [21] or Fallujah [22].

Wider historical, economic and global realities suddenly burst through the calm social surface. It is a shock-effect. But the shock is there for a purpose – and it is a purpose beyond the screen. A purpose *in* the world *in which* the screen exists. The world in which both my audience and I live our once-only lives. The only world, from which there is no escape.

It is a commonplace of Scriptwriting Guides and How To books that one must know the 'rules' in order to break them. I am not so sure that there are any *rules* but certainly there are *conventions*. The question to ask oneself is whether the convention serves your purpose as you take your audience on a particular journey. I am not an experimental writer; I do not introduce formal innovations and disturbances to see if they will work – I use them because they *do* work in terms of my intentions. Still less am I *avant garde* or elitist. Any viewer ought to be able to sit down and comprehend what I am doing with them by taking them on this journey. They might not *like* it, but that is quite another matter.

I am wary of much of the writing which goes on in the name of Writing or Script Theory. A book such as McKee's *Story*[23] has much to interest and offer the reader, as long as the reader remains aware that far from being the Universal Truth about storytelling in screenplays, McKee writes from a specific cultural, historical, class, and ultimately *ideological* position – a position which is hostile to the radical. I stand with Sartre, who posits that "the always new requirements of the social and the metaphysical involve the artist in finding a new language and new techniques".[24] In order to be radical, we must subvert, invert, extend and expose old and traditional methods of telling stories. In this way, we take the audience on a journey which subverts, inverts, extends and exposes new ways of human being.

Notes

[1] For example, Christopher Volger, *The Writer's Journey* (Pan, 1999).

[2] Edward Bond, *The Hidden Plot – Notes on Theatre and the State* (Methuen, 2000) p.20.

[3] This line is not in the published script, but can be clearly heard in the closing moments of the film, *Chinatown* (USA: 1974; director Roman Polanski; screenplay Robert Towne).

[4] Murray Sperber, "'Do as little as possible" Polanski's Message and Manipulation', *Jump Cut* No. 3. (USA: 1974), p.10.

[5] Samuel Beckett, *Waiting for Godot* (Faber and Faber, 1956), p.9.

[6] Christopher Booker, *The Seven Basic Plots – Why We Tell Stories* (Continuum, 2004), p.478.

[7] Ibid.

[8] " … and he rolled a great stone to the door of the sepulchre, and departed." Matthew, 27:60.

[9] Roland Barthes, *Mythologies* (Vintage, 1993), p.138.

[10] Ibid., p.139.

[11] " … to Generalise is to be an Idiot", William Blake, 'Annotations to Reynolds' in *Complete Writings* (Oxford University Press), p.451.

[12] Bond, p.172.

[13] Northrop Frye, *Fearful Symmetry – A Study of William Blake* (Princeton University Press, 1969), p.218.

[14] One woman who saw the play confessed to me that, having just been though a protracted and messy divorce procedure, she was rather taken by the idea of the reverse marriage ceremony. She made no comment on the castration.

[15] Jean-Paul Sartre, *What is Literature* (Routledge, 2001), p.61.

[16] Interestingly, in the light of this paper's subject, Martin Barker has suggested that it was the breaking of *dramatic convention* which, more than anything else, got the so-called 'video nasties' into legal hot water in the early 1980s: "The refusal of the heroic filmed conventions, of rounded characters, of encapsulated solutions, constituted the common core of the main 'nasties' … they disrupt the standard distance between film and audience in order to make ideas, rather than characters, their central focus." Martin Barker, 'Nasties: A Problem of Identification' in Martin Butler (ed.), *The Video Nasties – Freedom and Censorship in the Media* (Pluto Press, 1984), pp.117-18.

[17] I was later impressed that a writer I admire, Brett Easton Ellis, has taken a similar approach to portraying life in that decade in his seminal *American Psycho* (Paladin, 1991).

[18] Some people did, indeed, walk out.

[19] Again, some people did, indeed, laugh out loud.

[20] Bob Dylan 'In The Summertime', http://search.bobdylan.com/songs/summertime.html, site accessed 25.08.06.

[21] Abu Ghraib is the prison facility near Baghdad where coalition troops were found to be physically and sexually torturing Iraqi prisoners in 2003.

[22] Fallujah is a city in Iraq, subject to a massive bombardment by American forces in 2004, resulting in 4000-6000 Iraqi deaths, many of them civilians.

[23] McKee's book is choc-a-block with bourgeois conservative assumptions;

let me choose just one to illustrate how far someone like myself is likely to feel from his position: "Classical design is a mirror of the human mind", Robert McKee, *Story – Substance, Structure, Style and the Principles of Screenwriting* (Methuen, 1999), p.62.

[24] Sartre, p.17.

12

Did you hear the one about a comic's narrative?

Russell Kane

It is a truth universally acknowledged that a single man in possession of a good fortune must also be in want of a single man.

Why not begin with a real 21st-century style joke: not a good one, barely a witticism – but nonetheless a good point at which to begin my argument that narrative is an essential component in creating anything which even attempts to be funny.

That first italicised sentence is, of course, a bastardisation of Jane Austen's opener in *Pride and Prejudice*. The difference between 1806 and 2006 is that any single man who is well off is often assumed (by the post *Sex-in-the-City*, post-post-feminist, post-lad culture social porridge that lamentably feeds our wit) to be gay. It is not quite as funny if one says: a man who is not married but has lots of equity is probably gay. Indeed, it's borderline homophobic – but somehow the fusion of Austen and *Nuts*-magazine Britain seems to work, well – almost

This essay will gleefully break golden rules of mirth-academia, one of which is already infracted: Never Explain a Joke. Well, good! That is my cultural calling as a professional purveyor of mirth: to break rules, to take taboos and lick them offensively on the cheek.

In the following ejaculation (to use an Austenian noun) of ideas I will theorise why, and perhaps more controversially how, narrative is essential in elevating humour from the amusing to the hilarious. From observational jokes to political satire the conveyance of an amusing idea via a narrative framework of some kind is essential.

The inspiration for my theory comes from the un-funniest of all Austrians ever to have sported facial hair: Freud (actually Hitler was perhaps much less funny) who wrote one of the most influential books on jokes of all time: *Jokes and their Relation to the Unconscious*[1]. Once I have explored Freud, who unfortunately has a tendency to be drier than a pensioner's perm, we will move on to explore how the different comic genres use narrative in different ways; surely a crass, surreal joke about a squirrel that lives in the rectum of a giant needs no narrative: but, already, a story, albeit bizarre, begins, it breathes: who is this feculent rodent? Who is this tolerant yet sore Goliath? More of this later. Also, I will explore the idea of the comedian's 'set' – the total minutes of patter, as a cohesive narrative structure in itself, and reveal (unprofessionally on my part) some of the literary and storytelling tricks that bring the strands of a stand-up set to satisfying narrative convergence. I will finish by attempting to create a joke from scratch using all the Freudian and 'Kaneian' narrative tools we have explored.

So to begin with: Sigmund Freud. There is no substitute for reading the whole of this seminal work on the psychological techniques and processes of inducing chortles and guffaws; but here I will highlight some the essentials he discusses. As Freud did 100 years ago, I'll kick off with a not-great joke:

> There was a sign in the toilets that said 'please leave these toilets as you would like to find them' so I left a copy of *Playboy* and a Playstation in there.

In the grand tradition of Sigmund, this bon mot is hardly a side-splitter, but is good for flagging up some solid techniques. One device used a lot by modern stand-ups is a representation of the opposite; a pretend-embracing of the rules in order to subvert them by acting in a morally opposite manner. This is where the humour lies – it's just one of the techniques Freud discusses – but arguably the most important when considering narrative; the urge to surprise, twist and turn in storytelling – more important in joke-telling than in anything else. There are of course many other tricks Freud highlights, from the trusty pun to using the same word in different ways, but to the central thought: that narrative is vital in humour.

Freud's great achievement was not just categorising the infinitely different types of humour, but in theorising psychologically as to *how* they cause our brains to experience humour and compel us to laughter. This again is fundamental in positioning narrative as important in joking.

Freud has it that every time a human being has that light-bulb feeling, that sudden rush of mental energy, the sharp idea-having burn in the mind, nerve cells in the brain are rapidly connecting up like an electricity grid. The grid is called the synaptic network. Freud called this type of energy 'cathectic energy', and the moment of the light-bulb going DING, a 'cathexis'. There are many types of cathexes (the plural) – when solving a problem; when thinking of an idea for a short story; when a child recognises the face of an aunt or an uncle – all of these cause that rather satisfying rush of realisation: a cathexis. Jokes are no different. Freud concluded that cathexes cause a massive bolt of energy to be punched (the punch-line) at the moment of a single word, action or notion. This cathectic energy rushes into the part of the brain that deals with humour and the body reacts by releasing it as it has evolved to: through laughter. The greater the rush of energy, the greater the laughter.

One genre I work in which begins to cross the threshold into narrative, is the construction of comic similes like "drier than a pensioner's perm". When these two meanings of a word are quickly forced together, pleasurable energy courses through the mind and the cathexis prompts a chuckle, albeit inward. Another: "The other morning I woke up feeling rougher than the first draft of a student's essay."

My argument is that these techniques and many others become ten times as powerful when situated within a *story*, conveyed in *narrative*, beginning, as always, with strong character delineation. If we know the old lady, if we know the man's wit – there is more humanness, more character: Oscar Wilde's wit was drier than Margaret Becket's perm. It places more cathectic energy either side of the simile. It takes you on a storytelling journey, and at the moment of punchline, the punch of mental energy, there is more rush to be enjoyed; more laughter.

Within contemporary comedy there are many genres and sub-genres. Here are some of the main ones: observational, political, storytelling, one-liner, character-based, sketch, surreal. The genre I work in most frequently is what I like to call socio-observational – a blend of angry sociology and silly observations that allows to me to make pseudo-Marxian arguments with an air of *joie de vivre*; basically silliness which may or may not have a message, but if you don't want to look for the subtext, that's fine. I have large sections with jokes and ponderings upon the received differences between working-class and middle-class culture – and almost invariably my set becomes much more poignant when I enshroud my quips in narrative. At one point I talk about masculinity – how working-class culture functions on a reverse value system – how as a child my peers and I would compete to *fail* exams, to experiment with drugs, fight – failure was success. I bring in various characters, my father, my brother; places – my time at Middlesex University – and suddenly the observations and the humour are lifted into the realm of what I call the 'utterly human' – to be human is to be simultaneously involved in many narratives at once. Attached to each step of the joke is a spore of messy, real human emotion: what happens next? What's next in this sequence of real human life? When enough spores are attached 'BANG' – the punchline Buckeroos into existence. All that pent-up narrative-borne emotion is released in the only way a group of humans in a dark theatre know how: through the sweet sound of laughter.

Surreal comedy is very interesting to analyse in relation to the importance of narrative to comedy. Some of the most amusing things uttered by some of the funniest comics – Noel Fielding, Harry Hill et al, have large sections in their acts that seem to defy every convention of narrative. A five minute illogical rant about badgers or monkeys is, by its very unconventionality, hilarious. The pseudo-passionate speech about gherkins performed by a comedienne dressed as a pickled onion could reduce a room to helpless fits of giggles. How? Why? Well, the first possibility is that, if a piece of humour is far enough from the expected rules, parameters, and conventions it stops being wrong and starts to invert and get funny again. It is so *un*grounded in narrative that the free-floating nouns and adjectives flying past us like a Windows screensaver simply whisk us into a state of illogical hilarity. The image of a Sardine, compounds the subsequent image: The Queen on a BMX, compounds the next image of George W. Bush working in Burger King dressed as a Halal steak, and so on and so on. The gap between the recognised and experienced is far enough to produce a 'cathexsis'. After all, is this not how surrealist paintings remain powerful to this day? They defy any sort of lineal understanding. They make the brain think sideways.

Well, all this is true of course – but comedy, and indeed fiction, are primarily language arts (choreography and illustrations aside). Comedy *can* express itself visually, it can feel as though it has the textures of a painting, but ultimately it is a language art – and, there ARE some rules. The genius of the excellent surrealist comics is that there is, after all, a narrative thread holding it all together. The story about badgers from Harry Hill will always have some gloriously silly premise, and conclusion. The listener is knocked about on a pinball table of humour – but there is always a build, a cumulative effect that grows and swells toward a satisfying narrative release. All too often a very new comic will take the too-visual approach, come on dressed as a bottle of Tippex and express himself in disconnected word-parts. This gives him one minute of energy maximum, before this inefficient narrative battery burns itself out and you are left with silliness hanging in a void that all of a sudden looks desperate rather than funny – a half-hearted stab at creating funniness that in the end looks awkward and makes the comic feel a bit of a prat.

Political humour operates in exactly the same way. The comic who drops in that she hates George W. Bush will elicit a certain amount of reflex whooping, but to enter a fuller realm of humour, hypothetical narratives must be applied to the figures one wishes to mock. "Imagine George W. Bush trying to go shopping at Sainsbury's …" – the political figure we wish to pillory together is now plonked into the middle of a narrative. This premise can go anywhere, but is more than likely to end with the President making an embarrassing mistake in the vegetable aisle leading to some form of legume Armageddon. To simply have said "Bush can't even go shopping in Sainsbury's" would not be enough. A narrative, a rich farcical premise must draw us deeply in before laughter can be cathartically expelled.

Politicised narratives are not just for the laughter – they serve another function: the presentation of formerly hidden discourses to be reflected on in a new way. Twenty-five years ago, comics began to speak grittily about social class. Twenty-five years ago comics began to give racial equality a new narrative: humour; black and white people coming together to laugh at Richard Pryor's groundbreaking assaults on received racial wisdom. His powerful (and often blissfully offensive) narratives involving him, his women, and American white hegemony made people absorb racial discourse in a new way. That was a very powerful type of laughter. It would still have worked as detached observations, but when situated within, for example:

> A lot of white men look at me and say, why do ya always grab
> your dick when you're speaking ... and I say, well, I just wanna
> make sure you can't take it ... Shit! You taken ever'thing else!

In the past five or ten years the number of stand-ups with disabilities has mushroomed. The term 'stand-up' of course providing rich default humour for my colleagues who perform in wheelchairs. Let's take this as a premise and explore two hypothetical options:

> a) "Good evening, tonight I will perform stand-up comedy!"
> (and ironically gestures to wheelchair)
> b) "My mother said to me I would one day stand up, ladies
> and gentlemen, I didn't want to prove her wrong."

For me, the second with its warmth and narrative-lead into the punchline is much stronger – show the human, then the humour. Very new stand-ups often forget this. This narrative works in the same way as comedy about ethnicity – it provides a much-needed mainstreaming of a hidden discourse. People are oblivious to these narratives. The wheelchair they walk past everyday. The Iraqi refugee they barely acknowledge. What are their stories? Comedy can highlight these hidden narratives of life. It's the opportunity for a blind comic to convey a unifying piece of storytelling to a room full of randomly assembled people and bring them together in empathy, interest and finally, hopefully, laughter of recognition; for narrative, whilst enabling the audience to enjoy the perspective of The Other, a life-view of the seemingly alien, can paradoxically show the humanness, the sameness, the ordinariness of this world view. In any art form narrative always unifies, but in comedy it must; it simply must come together – and when it does, mutual laughter is its spiritual evidence.

The comedian's 'set' comes in various shapes and sizes, but the main accepted durations are: the five-minute 'open spot'; the ten-minute half-set; the fifteen minute; the 'paid' twenty; the forty-minute headline set; and the solo show. There are, of course, infinite variations on these, but mostly a comedian on his or her way to a gig will be about to perform one of those. In relation to narrative, they are all rather different. When I was very new to comedy, I would perform the five-minute open spot. This means in a club full of mildly drunk paying punters I would be sandwiched between two very experienced acts, each doing paid twenties, to get the chance to prove myself. Those first thirty or so gigs are not experiences I would like to repeat. Some, of course, went very well, others were disastrous. It is only in retrospect that I can appreciate the importance of overall structural narrative within a set. The tendency when I had five minutes to prove myself was to fall into 'and another thing' mode – just spouting three or four pieces of humour, that though in themselves may have had narrative, eroded the set's power by their discursiveness. If the entire piece that the comedian presents does not cohere, the set appears rehearsed, false and inorganic. It is hard within the five-minute format to stick to this. You don't want to hedge your bets, so you go scatter gun, hoping that if the seeds are cast wide enough some saplings of mirth will get through. But of course, less is more. The advice 'just talk about one thing' goes to the heart of the argument that narrative is fundamentally important in humour. Even if twenty jokes are to be told within that five-minute window, frame them in some sort of carrying, background narrative. This may be the narrative of who the comedian is: persona, mannerism, fleeting allusions to strange backgrounds – it is possible even for a one-liner gag-smith to do this. The audience feels less written at and more engaged with. Story is a human phenomenon, remember.

As the sets gets longer this gets easier and harder in equal measure! Once the heady day of actually getting paid to be funny arrives, it can be daunting. No comedian ever forgets the first time he or she was on stage for a whole 20 minutes and receiving cash as well. Ten seconds can seem like an aeon if a joke backfires. The point is not that the twenty-minute set should be one long story, or that it is some sort of vapid technique to build toward a sort of fake conclusion, no, but that it should carry itself from start to finish with a kind of narrative flow; a slick continuity. The random 'and another thing' mode becomes more intolerable, more unity-lacking in the twenty-minute set. I only have one joke about my Dad, yet I weave this paternal influence into all my angriest sections. It gives them a reason for being – a storytelling glue, pace. The laughter becomes a cumulative journey: narrative must progress, it must build.

The solo show is something else altogether. The modus operandi at the Edinburgh Festival is 'yes, be funny, but also, ideally, have an idea', a strong theme. Shows must begin with a compelling reason to be drawn into the story, and that story must carry the audience through the hour. Tangents and banter may abound, but, just as with a well-written essay, the question, the theme, the central proposition must always be returned to: The Story. Of course, it is not as black and white as this. I might not title my show, I may just use my name; but if, when the audience sits down to listen for an hour; if there is not some sort of narrative journey, an emotional story to plug into, the show will founder. I have experienced this myself. I thought that simply being high-energy, prancing around and telling jokes for an hour would be enough – but every time the show seemed to lag around the 35-minute mark. Gradually I began to work in more human touches, longer narrative strands that began in the opening five minutes and concluded in the final five – sections of light and shade, arcs that reflected the audience's energy level.

When I realised my overall topic, that was when the show really began to cohere, and *The Theory of Pretension* was born. This was the show I performed at The Edinburgh Festival 2006.

During the set there were also little narrative tricks and tools such as the 'call-back' – reusing or referencing an earlier punchline, the repetition induces the humour: I have a punchline early on about how people use silly suffixes to make their words more friendly (drinky-poos). I will then intentionally use this 'ypoos' suffix at the end of a word 20 minutes or so later. The false ending is another goodun – serving up what seems like the punchline, an unsatisfying, unfunny, ending, only to undercut it with the real ending a few moments later. These tricks, though, are only touches – the overall set must be 'killer' first.

The time now has come to break another of the rules and create a joke before your very eyes. As I type this sentence I genuinely have no idea what the joke will be about – it may not be amusing in any way, the exercise here is to try and use the tools of narrative to at least improve my impromptu effort at joke creation. As a primarily observational comic I shall pull an observation from yesterday's haul, the scribbled note reads thus:

> As my generation gets into its late twenties we are becoming typical consumers, but have the linguistic hangover of the dance scene. Product naming now has a tendency to reflect this. The Zanussi Kickback, The Bosch Techno Wave Microwave.

Well, there is certainly a funny-ish idea here. The potential for the creation of cathectic energy release, Freud would have it, is the gap between the everyday mundane, urban, middle-class drudgery of using one's microwave; and an attempt by the manufacturer to make that consumer still feel as though he is an eighteen-year-old dancing to Hard House in a field at The God's Kitchen dance festival. "I'm just popping my meal in my Techno microwave." Yes, the observation is building. Notice the slotting in of a pronoun "I'm" – the *story* has begun. "I'm" indicates our protagonist is on his own during this tale. Now, 'the meal for one': a good way of saying lonely and single, more powerful than saying lonely and single. Why – because there is more narrative packed into the imagery. To tell someone that you spend every night alone is too obvious, too being joked at – to use the image of the sad TV dinner adds textures, flavours, smells, tableaux to the minds' eyes. So, the narrative premise in which to frame this observation is that of a lonely stand-up comic, still egotistically trying to hang on to his night-clubbing kudos. Now to fuse it with the observation; the narrative, remember, only provides the structure and story: it must be correctly sutured (lovely word that) to the joking fabric, otherwise we will end up at the other end of the continuum and have all narrative and no joke: fine for fiction, but a red rag to drunken hecklers in a comedy club. Let's try a draft:

"Seen that latest microwave? The Zanussi Techno Pulse! 'Techno

Pulse!' I'm sick of fucking Zanussi [*a specific brand plus swearing: overly precise nouns plus Anglo-Saxon intensifiers are always funnier than generic descriptors, they provide little nounal stabs mid-sentence*] constantly trying to patronise me and make me think I'm still dance-scene-cool, even though I've totally sold out and live with pedigree cats in Clapham [*more narrative colour being dropped in: location, furry flatmates*] like I'm going to be microwaving my meal for one and then go and inhale poppers in the Habitat lounge while it all kicks off to thudding techno in my you-haven't-sold-out-and-become-a-lonely-internet-lonely-loser-comedian microwave."

Okay, there's the first draft. It is not even close to stage-ready – but you could try to make it funnier. The solution will always be in trying to find the correct narrative weights either side of the story. Perhaps a little more colour before the microwaving. Perhaps more detail about the meal itself. Is shepherd's pie funnier than lasagne? No, I would contend. Lasagne, glibly gestures as food adventurous – it's slightly more tragic, and it sounds funnier, the more awkward pronunciation the better. Bring in other characters. Do I dance with the cat? What's the cat's name? (My cat is actually called Keith – funny in itself, as the name is a bit too homo sapien.) And so on.

The point here, and of this whole chapter, is to illustrate the power of narrative in enriching the psychological processes of laughter. Start with the kernel of the humour and texturise with the things that make us human. Jokes and acceptable forms of shtick will change, fashions will come and go. In a relatively short period of time everything I have said will not be as funny as it was – because the things that are relevant will change, yet narrative is constant. From the earliest tribal leaders doing pre-linguistic routines about bagging an antelope, to postmodern invectives on Third World debt, the human story is always there, and will go on and on and on.

Life can be tricky sometimes, full of difficult plots, exciting beginnings, tragic endings: if one can have a fucking good giggle along the way, all the better.

Notes
[1] Sigmund Freud, trans. James Strachey, *Jokes and Their Relation to the Unconscious* (W.W. Norton and Company, 1972).

13

Swinburne's Duster Meets the King's Tailor
Helena Nelson

One hot day in August 1820, the 28-year-old poet Percy Bysshe Shelley set off to climb Monte San Pellegrino. He was spending some months at the Baths of San Giuliano with Mary, his wife, and their new baby. When he returned from the long slog, he was exhausted but also inspired. He immediately started a new poem and called it *The Witch of Atlas*.

Most people have heard of Shelley. Many people know *The Ode to the West Wind*, or *Ozymandias* (texts that still appear in anthologies and textbooks). *The Witch*, however, was never going to make it onto the school curriculum: too long, too weird. Even Mary (Shelley's faithful supporter) didn't like it – or rather, she surmised most readers wouldn't.

Nevertheless, Shelley stoutly defended its lack of 'story' in the preface. "Prithee, for this one time," he says irritably, "content thee with a visionary rhyme." He had done what he set out to do in his poem and was simply not prepared to abandon visions to "suit the popular taste". He had no intention of telling a story, having a sharp qualitative distinction in his own mind between story and poem. "A story," he later said in his essay *A Defence of Poetry*, "is a catalogue of detached facts, which can have no other connection than time, place, circumstance, cause and effect", whereas a poem "is the creation of actions according to the unchangeable form of human nature, as existing in the mind of the Creator, which is itself the image of all other minds." Phew.

Perhaps, after all, the last laugh was on Shelley. *The Witch of Atlas*, remains largely unread today. However, the story of its author's life has never failed to fascinate. This was a man who eloped with a 16-year-old schoolgirl, married her in Scotland, attempted an 'open marriage' (he wanted to share Harriet with his friend James Hogg), later left her for another teenage girl, Mary Godwin, and ran away again – to France this time, taking Mary's sister Claire with them. His short life was punctuated by death and disaster: his first wife drowned herself; several of his children died. Mary's sister Claire fell pregnant to his friend Byron – their child died too, at the age of five. And, of course, Shelley himself was drowned at only 30 in a boating accident. It was all desperately tragic – but so long ago that it is now a 'good story', in the journalistic sense. The truth is, human beings – no matter what Shelley said – relish stories, whether in poems, novels, biographies or plays. The love of story is so strong that it stretches fact into fiction all the time – and it can be the anecdotal tale, rather than the text, which draws the reader in.

For example, there's the story that Thomas Butts, friend to the poet William Blake, once visited Blake and his wife only to find them lying naked in the garden, declaiming passages from Milton's epic poem *Paradise Lost*. I remember first reading this when I was at school – a footnote in a little *Selected Blake* said something about it – and I feel ridiculously sure that my version described Blake and his wife unclothed in *an apple tree* reading Milton. This is unlikely to be true; I think it must be a false memory. Climbing apple trees without clothes on would be, at best, a risky business. But I like the idea so much – *Paradise Lost* naked in an apple tree – it's the story I want to remember. And it's what made me want to read Blake, and after that, also Milton's epic poem about Adam and Eve. In just the same way, once you know the story about Thomas Hardy's heart – you want to believe it so much that you cease to care whether or not it's true.

What story? Well, in 1928 when Hardy died of pleurisy, it was not all that unusual for the heart to be buried separately from the rest of the body (in this case it was destined for his first wife's grave). Hardy's heart – so the story goes – was placed temporarily on the kitchen table, where it was spotted and nabbed by the cat – which promptly ate it. Where do such stories come from? The supply seems to be endless, much of it stemming from sheer mischief – mischief and love of story, which sits at the origin of creativity itself.

Clearly it's not always the poem or play or novel that is the great creation. It may be the story of how it was made that captures the imagination. Or the author may be a character so interesting (like Shelley) that he starts to *be* the creation, to be several creations, in fact. If you're a writer yourself, you're caught up not only in what you're writing, but also in *how*: what went right, what went wrong, what interfered. In writing this essay, I have become part of the story of this book about story; and you, in reading it, have a part to play too – but more of that later.

Many people know Samuel Taylor Coleridge's story about the creation of his famous poem *Kubla Khan*. The marvellous lyric came to him, he said, in a dream. He woke up with the text complete in his head and began to write it down. He got as far as:

> I would build that dome in air
> That sunny dome! those caves of ice!
> And all who heard should see them there,
> And all should cry, Beware! Beware!
> His flashing eyes, his floating hair!
> Weave a circle round him thrice,
> And close your eyes with holy dread,
> For he on honey-dew hath fed,
> And drunk the milk of paradise.

and then there was a knock at the door, "a person on business from Porlock" interrupted him – and the rest is history. So the beautiful poem remains a fragment. Some people have suggested that Coleridge made up the whole thing because he got stuck and couldn't finish. It's possible. But if he did, what a marvellous story – and now the story is part of the poem, and the 'person from Porlock' is part of the mythology of literature. It is *the* ultimate story about interruption and it's a tale in which even the nameless person from Porlock acquires a literary status. That person has entered literature without even knowing that he (or she) was doing so, though only because Coleridge chose to tell the story. So far as we know, the Porlock visitor did not record his or her version of the event. But s/he could have done …

Because stories are not always created by well-known novelists, poets, dramatists. Sometimes, it is a less than literary friend who tells the tale – and because the subject has celebrity status, this too is published and passed on. In 1922, Clara Watts-Dunton's main claim to fame was her marriage to Theodore Watts-Dunton, a poet and critic whose own poems are now largely forgotten. However, he is still remembered as the friend of Algernon Charles Swinburne. Swinburne, who died in 1909, was once tremendously famous – sometimes even *in*famous for passionately risqué imagery, powerful flowing verse and a dangerously interesting lifestyle. Watts-Dunton saved Swinburne from a life of alcoholism by offering him a home; and after the poet's death, he even hid some chapters of his erotic sadomasochistic novel, *Lesbia Brandon,* to save the dead man from disgrace.

Watts-Dunton's wife Clara, regarded Swinburne as a very great writer indeed – so much so that she compiled *The Home Life of Swinburne*, recording details of the poet's domestic existence with loving particularity. In so doing, she won herself a small part in Swinburne's story, which is, in itself, part of the story of 19th-century English poetry. Perhaps a reader coming to Swinburne's verse today may not find it immediately attractive – it is too ornate, flowery and *long* to suit modern taste. But once you know about Swinburne's duster, suddenly he becomes a whole person – idiosyncratic – prone to a spot of obsessive-compulsive disorder – definitely worth making a film about. On the one hand, we have his reputation for excessive drinking and sado-masochistic writing; on the other, we see his passion for – dusting. On entering Swinburne's room, good Mrs Watts-Dunton couldn't help noticing the red-and-yellow-checked duster which always hung in the same prominent place over the back of a cane chair. The great poet had to have the duster in sight at all times, due to his "horror of even touching a dusty book". Before handing a volume to a friend, "he would first of all see that not a speck was on it … duster in hand, going carefully over the edges and cover to satisfy himself that all was as it should be". There he is – Swinburne the 19th-century poet, alive and kicking, his fear of dust as memorable as his incomplete *Lesbia Brandon.*

There's no doubt that Clara Watts-Dunton won herself a toe-hold in literature simply by writing her memoirs down. But stories are not always passed on in writing. During an ordinary conversation, my friend Stewart Eglin told me a tale about the Scottish poet Hugh MacDiarmid who, in the early 1970s, came to read his poems in Kirkcaldy, Fife. MacDiarmid famously led the Scottish literary renaissance of the 20th century. Apart from being a magnificent poet, he was a Communist, a Scottish nationalist and a tried-and-tested whisky drinker. After the Kirkcaldy reading, a group of 20 to 30 people (including my friend Stewart) repaired to the nearby Station Hotel where alcohol fuelled lively talk about use of Scots in poetry. Soon discussion flared into argument, and argument escalated into rage. Was the Scots used by MacDiarmid the real article? Or was it "not proper Scots" as some people present asserted? Everyone – an entire room full of men – was drunk, to varying degrees. Quickly the scene degenerated into something worthy of the Wild West, with glasses literally hurled across the room. Alarmed, Stewart Eglin sought refuge behind a table which had been propped up like a shield on the floor. He found a man already hiding there – no other than the great poet himself buttoned into his duffel coat, hood pulled over his head in protection. Stewart crouched down beside him. MacDiarmid didn't seem unduly alarmed. "The boys are in good form tonight," he remarked. Eventually, both men crept from the shelter of the table to the back door of the hotel, taking the story with them. And here it is, duly handed over. What will you do with it?

Because anybody can be part of the story. Clara Watts-Dunton, Stewart Eglin, me, you – we are all potential narrators – grabbing the baton in the race and running with it. All you have to do is be there, see what is going on, and then tell someone – or write it down. Stories are a way of saving a little bit of reality from being lost, and they can arise from the most unlikely things. Even the making of a poem can be a story. Let me tell you about Stan and Penny. Two years ago, I agreed with fellow poet and e-zine editor George Simmers to write a two-handed poem[1], each of us taking the voice of one character. It seemed like fun – something a bit different. George started it off. He devised a situation in which his character (Stan) was to contact someone he was once at school with – a sort of 'Friends Reunited' idea. Subsequent exchanges were to take place by email, both in the story and in reality. Stan's first message was a chatty, friendly sonnet. I replied as an irate Penny:

> Good God, it's Stan. You've got a bloody cheek.
> You saw me on the underground last week.
> YOU KNOW YOU DID.

At the end of her first message, Penny tells Stan to "piss off", which of course he did not. Instead it was the start of an emotional cut-and-thrust in which all sorts of facts were revealed about these two characters and their previous relationship: they had once been in love; Stan had lost all their money on a dodgy business; Penny had given birth to triplets which Stan thought were his but Penny denied; George had a new 21-year-old Estonian wife; Penny had a lesbian lover. And so on. On one level it was a sort of competition between George and me (because we were enjoying ourselves). But in another way, Stan and Penny became curiously real, both of them outrageous in various ways.

As the exchange went on, George and I also became more and more dramatic with the poetic forms we used to express strong feeling. For example, when I went into double-dactyls (which always sound comical), George replied in a pastiche of Ginsberg (long ranting lines). We never knew what was going to come back or how, and as time went on, each of us became more and more involved. At several points I grew quite agitated as George developed a twist I hadn't anticipated and I can honestly say that for several weeks I was thinking about Penny most of the time (instead of other things I was meant to be doing). The highpoint was when Stan wrote to say he'd read in the paper that Penny's house had been burned down by her lesbian lover Amanda – who had died in the flames. I phoned my son. *What shall I do? He's killed Amanda!* I won't reveal what happened in the end, only that it was completely cathartic for both of us, and after it was over, life felt remarkably boring.

Once *Re: United* was complete, instead of publishing it as a book or on the web, we invited interested readers to take part in an experiment in which they received a Stan or Penny email every few days, in the same order in which they'd been written. At this stage, it was gratifying to find that readers became equally wound up about what would happen next. To this day, I miss the excitement of not knowing the next twist in the plot – because telling a story is one of the most exciting things I know, and the next most exciting thing is reading that story – when it works. There's a kind of energy spinning from the words.

Re:United was a complete story and it was a comedy. It's not, however, the only poem I've written which tells a story. Many of my serious poems do just that. I've been writing about a middle-aged couple called Mr and Mrs Philpott[2] for nearly ten years now. I have no idea where this couple came from – somewhere in the depths of my subconscious perhaps, since the Philpott poems are not autobiographical, although each of the characters reminds me of parts of people I know. As the poems have continued to arrive (a new one pops into my head every six months or so), I've found I gradually know more about the Philpotts, and sometimes my knowledge increases before the poem arrives. For example, when I wrote the poem called 'Preserves', which is about Mrs Philpott's jam-making year, I already knew that Mr Philpott's first wife had died in December – and that is why, in the 'Preserves' poem, December and January are "the bleaker days". The poem about that death came much later.

I have other poems – not about the Philpotts – which arise from my own life-story or other people's. Often they only hint at what has happened or will happen: they work more by suggestion than explicit narrative, sometimes as part of an attempt to understand something that can't be fully understood. Or they hinge on a metaphor which is never explained fully: it's up to the reader to decide what it might mean. In my view there needs to be a bit of mystery at the heart of a poem, an element that is alluring for both writer and reader. Readers start to be involved when they get interested in the puzzle – perhaps because they closely relate to the situation, perhaps because they *don't*. However, each reader can only tackle the mystery for her/himself and one reading doesn't have to be exactly the same as another. The reader has a role to play. And that's as it should be.

Naturally I will conclude with a story, this time from a different genre again. Although this is a written version, I first heard *The King's Tailor* from the marvellous Scots storyteller, Stanley Robertson. Robertson is one of the travelling folk and his story, drawn from an ancient oral tradition, was delivered with inimitable style and gesture – and in places the audience was invited to join in, which you can't really do here. However, I will do my best, since the story of *The*

King's Tailor is close to my heart. It says much of what I have tried to say – in a kind of metaphor which I'll leave it to you to 'read'.

The Story of the King's Tailor

Once upon a time there was a king who had the finest tailor in the world. The tailor was so talented that the king was envied for his beautiful clothes everywhere he went. No-one had ever seen such dazzling designer garments, made with such subtlety and care. One day the king decided it was time to reward his tailor for the wonderful service he had given him. So he said to the tailor: "Forget the next garment you're due to make for me. I want you to make something for *yourself.* I want you to make yourself a beautiful coat. Get the best – the very best – material you can find. Never mind the cost. I will foot the bill."

The tailor was deeply moved. He had very few clothes, and those he had were nothing to write home about. So he did exactly as the king said. He ordered some amazing material from China. It was shot through with real gold thread, and its vivid colours flashed and glittered, even in the half light of his studio. It cost a fortune – and the king paid the bill without so much as raising an eyebrow. For several days the tailor closed his doors, sat inside and worked on the coat using every last scrap of the precious cloth. And after a week, it was done.

Early one morning, the tailor opened his door and walked out into the streets of the city wearing his new coat. It was very long, nearly touching the ground, and it had a high collar and gorgeous sleeves. Suddenly the little man seemed taller and more dignified. The colours flashed in the sun, dazzling the townspeople. As he walked down the road towards the market, they all gasped and cried out, "What a magnificent coat!!" And as he walked back up the road with his groceries, all the people sighed with envy and cried out in chorus, "Could you not make *me* a coat like that?"

"Very sorry," said the king's tailor politely. "No more material."

The tailor continued to wear his magnificent coat for years. Whenever he went out, he put it on, and wherever he went people were astounded. The coat was so beautifully made that it lasted and lasted and lasted. But eventually, it began to show signs of damage. The elbows were wearing thin. One day a hole appeared near the hem, and the collar started to fray. The tailor gave it a long, hard look. He knew he couldn't wear it any more: its life was over. He sighed a long, long sigh, bundled it up, threw it in the bin and went back to work.

But as he worked, light kept catching on the gold thread on the discarded coat in the bin. And each time the flash of gold caught his attention, he was distracted and sad. Suddenly he got up, pulled the coat out of the bin again and grabbed the scissors. "I can make something of this yet," he said. "At least I *think* I can." For three days and three nights he worked. And when he was done, he had made a neat waistcoat out of his old coat. It was a wonderful waistcoat: stylish, neatly cut and sparkling like stars in the night sky.

Early one morning, the tailor opened his door and walked out into the street, wearing his new waistcoat. The colours flashed in the sun, dazzling all the people. As he walked down the road towards the market, they all gasped and cried out, "What a wonderful waistcoat!!" And as he walked back up the road with his groceries, all the people sighed with envy and said, "Could you not make *me* a waistcoat like that?"

"Very sorry," said the king's tailor politely. "No more material."

For years and years, the king's tailor wore his wonderful waistcoat. It was beautifully made, of course, so it lasted and lasted. But one day, he took a long, hard look at it and sighed. The material at the back (where he leaned against his chair) was wearing thin. Most of the gold thread had lost its sparkle. "No use," he said. "It has to go." And he bundled it up, threw it in the bin and went back to his work.

But as he worked, light kept catching on a bit of gold thread in the discarded waistcoat. And each time the flash of gold caught his attention, he was distracted and sad. Suddenly he got up, pulled the waistcoat out of the bin again and grabbed the scissors. "I can make something of this yet," he said. "At least I *think* I can." All night he worked. And when he was done, he had made a tie out of his discarded waistcoat. It was a terrific tie: elegant, well-shaped and glistening like a fish as it jumps out of the water.

Early next morning, the tailor opened his doors and walked out into the street, wearing his new tie. The colours flashed in the sun, dazzling all the people. As he walked down the road towards the market, they all gasped and cried out, "What a terrific tie!!" And as he walked back up the road with his groceries, all the people sighed with envy and said, "Could you not make *me* a tie like that?"

"Very sorry," said the king's tailor politely. "No more material."

For years and years, the king's tailor wore his terrific tie. It was beautifully made, of course, and a tie can last and last. But one day, as he put the tie around his neck, he realised that the material was about to break. He wouldn't be able to knot it again. That tie was scuppered. "No use," he said. "It has to go." And he bundled the tie up, threw it in the bin and went back to his work.

As he worked, light kept catching a few gold fibres on the discarded tie. And each time a flicker of gold caught his attention, he was distracted and sad. Suddenly he jumped up, pulled the tie out of the bin and grabbed the scissors. "I can make something of this yet," he said. "At least I *think* I can." For three hours he worked. And when he was done, he had made a button out of his discarded tie. It was a brilliant button: a neat circle of glistening material, and it shone at the neck of his faded blue shirt like a new moon.

Early next morning, the tailor opened his doors and walked out into the street, wearing his old shirt and his brand new button. The colours flashed in the sun, dazzling all the people. As he walked down the road towards the market, they all gasped and cried out, "What a brilliant button!!" And as he walked back up the road returning from the market with his groceries, every single person sighed with envy and said, "Could you not make *me* a button like that?"

"Very sorry," said the king's tailor politely. "No more material."

For years and years, the king's tailor wore his brilliant button. It was cleverly made, of course, and a button can last well. But one day, as he took off his shirt, he realised the colours on his button had faded miserably. All the gold thread was worn away. The button was finished. "No use," he said. "It has to go." So he plucked the button off his shirt, threw it in the bin and went back to work.

But as he worked, he sighed and sighed. He was getting old and there wasn't much to look forward to any more. Suddenly, a tiny sparkle caught his eye from the bottom of the bin. One speck of gold gleamed on the back of the button. He leapt up and grabbed the button out of the bin. "I can make something of this yet," he said. "At least I *think* I can." For a week and a day he worked. And when he was done, he had made something new out of his old button.

What do you think the king's tailor had made?

He had made this story.

Notes

[1] Snakeskin Webzine, ed. George Simmers http://homepages.nildram.co.uk/~simmers/. Link to *The Re: United Poems* is on the home page.

[2] The Philpott poems in *Starlight on Water* (Rialto Press, 2003).

14

Sea of Stories

Graeme Harper

1

Diving into the surf, the boy, brown and skinny as a stick, claws
downward, against the tow of the break. His arms, frogging at the
elbows, are uncoordinated, flaying, without finesse; his hands are
mere wishes of flippers, grebe desires not cormorant reality. And yet
he moves. Downward.

Around him there is nothing, and everything. Nothing, because
here at first he can see only the churn of sand and the wisps of currents.
Indecipherable. Or the slide of something? Alert! A fish. A ray. Deep
denizen! Or perhaps nothing? Merely some scoop of a human limb,
as paddlers behind him wade, and stumble, against the surge. And
he, moving downward, only claws away from them. Toward no space.
Empty space. Or is it?

Here is nothing, and everything. The boy knows this. Why else
would he be clawing so determinedly downward? Beyond the
clouding of waves – the sand in unfathomable motion, tangled
glimpses of human limbs, muted screeches, muffled shouts. Beyond
this, something far greater.

He feels the colder water. It wafts across his belly. His back. His
flexing thighs. Moves through him. For a moment he wonders how
warmth and cold can entangle this way; how one can keep itself
from the other; why now there is not simply a tepid wash. Then,
before this thought is complete, the threads of warm water are gone

and he is immersed in cold.

A breath taken away goes where? Into the self? Into oblivion? Is it never taken? Or does it lie in wait?

Only for one stroke does the boy slow down. But the cold alerts him and this pause is indication of something new. The cloud of sand and wads of weed are a curtain drawn back. A rock emerges, cupped by a mound of white sand, brown and ridged. Then a crab: darting from beneath the rock and shooting white across the sea bed. Ahead, where once there was just black, there is a shaft of light, flowing with jewels. And then another shaft. And another. A new light replaces the old; but this new light is golden, intentional, fresh.

Here is everything, and nothing. Having clawed his way now to a spot beyond the break, the boy floats, suspended, looking back toward nothing, held in place by the spectacle, both in and out of place and time, no pain of breathing, no jumble of limbs, no muffled shouting rush.

2

The sea is the subject and source of many stories. Our interaction with it is also a wonderful metaphor for our interchange and exchange with stories: those aspects of struggle and suspension, of spectacle and personal awe, of nothing and everything. The philosopher and 1927 Nobel Laureate, Henri Bergson, once spoke about the function of the intelligence being to 'establish relations', and it seems clear this too is one of the primary functions of stories: to establish relations in the same way as the sea has a relation with the history of human kind — sometimes borne out of observation, sometimes out of direct active experience, sometimes out of recollection, memory, myth, geographic reality or even unexpected natural intrusion! And this metaphoric link travels even further than this.

Bergson also made a distinction between the 'intelligence' and 'intellect' by suggesting that while the intelligence is capable of dealing with the world in fluid sea-like motion – that is, *in process* – the intellect can only deal with it by breaking it up into smaller chunks and stopping it dead[1]. That is, the intellect needs to separate and compartmentalize in order to analyze and grasp; whereas the intelligence, less formally celebrated in places like universities and colleges though it is, is capable of analyzing and grasping without the need for separation, compartmentalization and stasis. Thus, the intellect requires that a naturally moving, evolutionary situation be rendered something it isn't, whereas the intelligence works in the same way as actual, lived experience.

Telling stories and consuming them seems, in that Bergsonian sense, an act of considerable human intelligence, not a narrow, compartmentalizing act of the intellect.

3

Of course, what precedes here is a highly paraphrased version of some of Bergson's thought. It brings together ideas from his *Time and Free Will: An Essay on the Immediate Data of Consciousness* (1889), *Matter and Memory* (1869) and *Creative Evolution* (1907). Other Bergsonian ideas include the notion of consciousness as a memory, which is a useful conceptual ideal for differentiating between those acts that appear to inform only mundane but very necessary motor functions (e.g. remembering not to leave the tap running after washing prevents a bathroom flood!) and those that appear to have a deeper, more selective element. Bergson's pursuit of the nature of this 'Pure Memory' examines why mental image and physical stimulus do not always correspond, suggesting consciousness is full of deliberations and human free thinking.

Similarly, Bergson challenges ideas about time, suggesting that 'scientific time' (i.e. the time depicted on clocks and watches and referred to in timetables and schedules) is not the time of experience, noting that there is a need to recognise and work with humankind's internal temporal intuition, that real, lived time that provides access to, and is determined by, different modes of knowledge to that knowledge called 'scientific'.

If the stick-like boy, dripping wet and gasping for air, is now returning to the gaggle of parents and kids gathered on colourful towels on the sand and Henri Bergson is, at least metaphorically, back in his oak-panelled room at the Collège de France, still something must remain of their appearances here. Something, that is, about stories. Something more than merely a discussion of narrative.

4

In Structuralist terms, as many literary theoreticians will quickly point out, the 'what' of a narrative is called Story, and the 'how' of a narrative is called the Discourse. This, of course, is a very specific usage, and it is one I've taught many university students with the demonstrative tone and gleaming eye of the true zealot — and then, afterwards, questioned myself to distraction with regard to whether I meant what I'd been teaching. I really must do something about my intrusive conscience!

If 'story' might be considered in that way – as the 'what' – then my own time in the world suggests 'stories' (perhaps, it appears, something very different to 'story') are the entwining of the 'what' and 'how' and not reducible to such simple binaries as the Structuralist schema might suggest. Stories so brilliantly recall for us that the world is made up of actions, thoughts, events, structures and functions and we, as the human occupants of the world, are the recorders of this, the sole creative writing inhabitants, who can approach and record the whole wild sea of existence, in parts, in places, in its mad, mad entirety.

This assessment might appear far too casual and raw, too random and ill-formed. And yet, that too is the essence of the point here. The world, in summary, is made up of actions, events, thoughts and materials that do not conform to structural or functional rules. These are what we often refer to as the 'unintentional' and the 'fortuitous'. They meet the individually emotional, the dispositional, the psychological, and they occur in and around the realms of the formal, the intentional and the structured. To ignore this intersection of organized and 'disorganized' or 'unorganized' existence quite obviously falsifies the nature of the world, and gives credence to notions about it that take us further away from our humanity. And yet, how often does ignoring the intersection of the personal or individual and the holistic or societal reflect an attempt to narrow down and grasp the nature of our existence? How often is this act – done because of entirely laudable motives – merely a matter of looking for some kind of 'handle on things' that might assist us in understanding phenomenon or events? And how often, in fact, are stories far better tools for doing exactly that; far better, far more accurate, far more connected with our actual human lives than any analysis predicated on structures and functions often defined without reference to our dispositions, intentions and emotions?

5

Emmanuel Le Roy Ladurie seems to know this!

Emmanuel Le Roy Ladurie (born 1929) is a French historian working mostly on the history of the French peasantry in the 15th to 18th-centuries. His most famous book possibly remains *Montaillou,* published in 1975. In this book, Le Roy Ladurie uses the notes of a member of The Inquisition, Jacques Fournier, the Bishop of Pamiers from 1318 to 1325, to reconstruct the history of a small French village during that time. Others of his books – *Jasmin's Witch* (1987), for example, or *Carnival in Romans* (1980) – perform similar miracles of discovery and of storytelling, using available records to make some sense of the lives of people alive almost seven hundred years previous.

When I was first led to Le Roy Ladurie's work by a very fine lecturer in Social and Economic History at the University of New England (in Armidale, north-western New South Wales, Australia), I was amazed. Was this history? Was this truth? Could I quote this in an academic essay in Social History, where the demands of veracity and at least giving it your best postgraduate shot at revealing 'actuality', determined not only your grasp of the subject but your likelihood of passing your course?! It turned out that not only *could* I quote Le Roy Ladurie, the suggestion was that I *should* quote him. And not only Le Roy Ladurie either. His was (and is) the kind of historiography sometimes referred to as 'microhistory', sometimes mentioned in the same breath as 'total history', sometimes theoretically underpinned by more complex terms like 'relational-structurism' and 'structurationism'. Names that are heard in the company of Le Roy Ladurie include Fernand Braudel, Anthony Giddens, E.P. Thompson and Marc Bloch, among others. These are historians and sociologists who view historiography as an act encompassing and recounting the ordinary lives of individuals, their emotive and dispositional acts and ideas, the mentalités (or psychology of an epoch) and the importance, form and type of actual human agency. Some of them – Le Roy Ladurie, for example – are connected with The Annales School of historical writing named after the French scholarly journal *Annales d'histoire économique et sociale* (renamed in 1994 as *Annales. Histoire, Sciences Sociales*). The historiographers of the Annales School have actively incorporated social scientific methods in their writing of history, and in doing so have tended to emphasize the recording of individual's lives, as well as the lives of political parties or economic phenomenon or of societies.

All of this has a relationship with the importance of stories – but not in the same way that the literary critics mentioned earlier might discuss them.

6

History is a series of stories. This I worked out a very long time before discovering Emmanuel Le Roy Ladurie and his ilk. Being inclined toward the writing of stories, this was a fact that led me to enjoy studying History at high school, even if I felt I should more enjoy studying literature. Eventually, I topped my final school year in history, won a nicely gold-embossed certificate (which, being a hoarder, I still have somewhere) and went on to study for a Bachelor's degree jointly in English and history. Hedging my bets. Why?

Simply, because until disovering Le Roy Ladurie and his ilk, history, as presented to me at least, was far too much of a series of orchestrated facts. Even when these facts were presented with historiographical provisos – e.g. the First World War was said to have been partly caused by the assassination of Austrian Archduke Franz Ferdinand, but then it was noted that some debate arose as to the significance of this act, and maybe it didn't 'cause' the First World War, as such, at all – even with such provisos history seemed, nevertheless, to be recalled by historians as a series of large acts, impacting in more or less communal ways on a more or less significant group of people who formed the basis of a more or less established or evolving set of social and cultural structures of functions and all made up the more or less 'true' accounts of history as we understood it.

I smelled a rat!

Speaking metaphorically, this rat had the same smell as that which the swimming boy detected when he dove beneath the waves of the crowded beach and, leaving behind what was the established practice of his friends and family, splashing and squealing and surfing the waves, headed toward a cold wash of seeming nothingness. Nothing and everything. Because this is the same sort of feeling those examining the old politics-focused, male-orientated histories of the pre-1960s felt when they noticed that certain groups of people, and some key individuals, were missing from these records of the past. Women, for example! Those old patriarchal histories of the western world, mostly written before the 1960s, spent little time on the individuals of divergent social classes, seemingly 'powerless' social positions, or supposedly 'peripheral' personal and cultural ideals. Yet, in so many ways, those histories written narrowly around 'politics and great men' seemed to provide everything in the way of constructed argument and well-formed explanation. Even women at very least *appeared* to enjoy them! Even those left out of them for cultural reasons (not being western, for example), or for reasons of their supposed irrelevance to the great historical movements at work around them, were eagerly reading them! And yet, by the time I encountered these histories in any kind of professional sense, there were a great many more knowledgeable people than I who felt that even the eminence of some of the historians who had produced these works did nothing to appease that sense that something was missing, something was not being said, something was wrong.

When *Montaillou* and the works of other historians and sociologists with relational-structurist or structurationist ideas first came into view for me, I was struck immediately by the relaxed nature with which the writers were working. These were comfortable pieces of writing. Not comfortable in that sense of being unchallenging – indeed, some of these histories were exceedingly complex. But comfortable in that sense of exuding understanding and approaching truth with careful attention to the other possibilities lurking nearby. The writers seemed both aware of the existence of other stories and confident in exploring their own contributions.

This is the 'everything' the boy encountered in the sea. I guess I could carry the marine metaphor far too far here! And I guess, just for fun, I will — fun being one of our most underrated modes of knowledge acquisition. So, metaphor to the fore: if you splash around on the surface of the sea, ride it a little, stare at it long and hard, but only from one viewpoint (your own), and only as far as your own encounters with it can encompass, then how at all is it possible to believe that you know a lot about it or, in fact, why would you want to think that? Similarly, who might know more about it: the oceanographer, the sailor, the scuba-diver or the surfer? If you were stuck out in the Pacific, bobbing around on a length of shiplap, a broken plank from some once highly-varnished clinkered yacht, now sunken way beneath you, with which of these experts would you rather be marooned? Impossible to tell, perhaps! You end up falling back on stereotypes (e.g. 'Oh please don't let it be the surfer, those guys never take anything seriously.') Equally, it is probably the case that few of us would say 'None of them. I'd rather just be alone'.

The great vastness of our own human ocean means that the majority of people would rather spend some time with other humans, even if there are some people who would prefer that time spent to be infrequent. Likewise, despite the friendly reputations of dolphins and whales, most of us would rather be within earshot of another person if set adrift. What the Annales Historians, and those like them, seemed immediately to offer – from the moment of my first, innocent reading of their work – was a sense in which their telling of the stories that constituted some portion of history was an amalgamation and intersection of other stories, an amalgamation of small facts and an intersection of them to create a story with considerable truth-value. What struck me, soon after, was that when a sociologist like Anthony Giddens talked of the importance of human agency he was reinstating fortuitousness and unpredictability in the story of society, highlighting the ways in which human emotions and dispositions, individual psychology and group dynamics have as much impact on our world as seemingly 'in-human' structures, 'fixed' economic and political systems and the totalizing functions of nations or cultural movements. This reinstating provides a far truer depiction of the true nature of human exchange, between humans, and between humans and the World around them.

7

Stories are our primary mode and a means of exchange. How many times have you been somewhere and met someone for the first time and not known who they were *in essence* or how they felt about those things you care deeply about? How many times have you been enlightened simply by the exchange of a story or stories? For example, the new work colleague who, in the embarrassing silence when you two share a lift journey, suddenly blurts out a story about how trying to get his kids to school while also trying to find the right bus to catch to his new job caused him to forget his office swipe card. And you recall, if not verbally than certainly in your own mind, that time you got stuck out of your hotel room in Copenhagen, during one summer holiday, because you left your key in your rucksack, stuck up on the fourth floor of a tiny Danish *pensione*. You both look up into the opposite corners of the lift, smiling, not quite connecting, but something, if merely a declaration of self, or a celebration of possibility, or even a recollection of vulnerability, shifts the stiff air, and thus two people have suddenly *met*.

Are stories, then, simply a point of contact?

Perhaps. Perhaps, though, like the kiss or the handshake they carry more complex coding. A story might declare a mutual interest, but it might equally establish parameters. It might find a way through the warm terrain of attraction or, though it is perhaps too strong a word in most instances (thankfully!), the dank, dark terrain of repulsion. Stories set up ideas and ideals, if sometimes only to take them back down again. Stories speculate. Oh, yes, boy, do stories speculate! The speculative 'what if?' component of a story is one of its most important outreaching elements. I'd return you, momentarily, to the tight lift space with your new colleague and point to the 'what if this was me?' element of the exchange. This is a coming together of past (yours) and present (his). It does not necessarily involve sympathy (you thinking: 'Hey, no problem, I have a pass card. I can get him into his office, poor guy') but it certainly involves empathy (you thinking: 'My God, Copenhagen was cold in August. I mean: how cold was the place?! And how unimpressed was that hotel porter?! But what were we supposed to do: it was the middle of the night?')

Empathy and story writing and story consuming seem so entwined as activities as to be inseparable. The point of contact here is not necessarily reminiscence, nor even direct experience, but it is the kind of contact that Henri Bergson noted in considering what lived experienced produces in terms of individual human memory, the "pure memory" of humankind's internal temporary intuition.

8

Does this give us any real clues to what makes a great story?

I think it does. But it also alerts us to the fundamental problem of dealing with that important question only by giving an answer concerned with *the surface of it*. If I have to read another book on creative writing that declares that a story should have a beginning, a middle and an end, involve some kind of 'inciting action' and contain a version of a denouement, I'll run screaming into the street! Inevitably, those very instructions involve those doing the instructing adding 'of course, there are exceptions'.

Indeed there are! It is the exceptions that alert us to the fact that such descriptions of stories as those above are starting at the wrong place. The achievement of stories is such that, firstly, the nature and type of the knowledge and experience they contain defines their structure and form, *not* the other way around.

A great story, despite the binary suggestions around 'story' and 'discourse' is almost certainly one which combines the 'what' and the 'how' of its makeup in an indivisible way, relating most accurately the ways in which our understanding of the idea of story and narrative are equally indivisible. I'm reminded of a moment when, at an academic conference, a speaker declared that 'birth to death is our primary human *narrative*', only to remind me immediately that 'birth to death' is, and certainly should be, our most fundamental human *story*.

Secondly, the nature of, and purpose of, stories is such that what they contain in subject matter is the product of a very individual exchange, producer to consumer – even if that individual exchange is defined by cultural or societal norms, conventions and conditions, and even if that production and consumption involves group acts.

A great story can be one that provides an empathetic connection between many people; but it is more likely to be one that is a great story to some, a pretty good story for others, and an average story for a bunch more. A great story might well be the meeting between individual experience, knowledge and understanding and another individual's experience, knowledge and understanding. That, I can confidently predict, will be its constitution of 'greatness'.

Thirdly, a great story will behave as if it is aware, as Henri Bergson was aware, that some things we have done in the world, thinking beings that we are, have been about falsifying notions of lived experience in order to try and grasp it. We compartmentalize, we structure and place strictures on the true nature of time and space. We stop phenomenon dead in order to try and understand them. And, in all that, we don't entirely grasp things; we don't understand them any better; and we don't give credence to the importance of creative human agency. But stories reassert something of the true nature of existence; they bring to us connections and swim down as if toward nothing, only to find everything exists in a fluid, moving realm. It is stories that give breath back, or provide breaths never taken; it is stories that look inward to the shore and outward to the unfathomable, at the same time.

Notes

[1] H. Bergson, *Creative Evolution*, orig. published 1907. L'Evolution créatrice (University Press of America, 1983), p.152.

Bibliography

H. Bergson, *Time and Free Will: An Essay on the Immediate Data of Consciousness*, originally published 1889. Essai sur les données immédiates de la conscience (Dover Publications, 2001).

H. Bergson, *Matter and Memory*, orig. published 1896. Matière et mémoire (Zone Books, 1990).

H. Bergson, *Creative Evolution*, orig. published 1907. L'Evolution créatrice (University Press of America, 1983).

A. Giddens, *The Constitution of Society. Outline of the Theory of Structuration* (Polity Press, 1984).

E. Le Roy Ladurie, *Montaillou: Cathars and Catholics in a French Village, 1294-1324* (Scolar Press, 1978).

E. Le Roy Ladurie, *Carnival in Romans* (George Braziller, 1979).

E. Le Roy Ladurie, *Jasmin's Witch* (George Braziller, 2000).

MORE GREENWICH EXCHANGE BOOKS

Also by Maggie Butt:

Lipstick
Lipstick is Maggie Butt's debut collection of poems and marks the entrance of a voice at once questioning and self-assured. She believes that poetry should be the tip of the stiletto which slips between the ribs directly into the heart. The poems of *Lipstick* are often deceptively simple, unafraid of focusing on such traditional themes as time, loss and love through a range of lenses and personae. Maggie Butt is capable of speaking in the voice of an 11th-century stonemason, a Himalayan villager, a 13-year-old anorexic. When writing of such everyday things as nylon sheets, jumble sales, X-rays or ginger beer, she brings to her subjects a dry humour and an acute insight. But beyond the intimate and domestic, her poems cover the world, from Mexico to Russia; they deal with war, with the resilience of women, and, most of all, with love.
Maggie Butt is head of Media and Communication at Middlesex University, London, where she has taught Creative Writing since 1990.
2007 • 72 pages • ISBN 978-1-871551-94-5

LITERATURE & BIOGRAPHY

Matthew Arnold and 'Thyrsis' *by Patrick Carill Connolly*
Matthew Arnold (1822-1888) was a leading poet, intellect and aesthete of the Victorian epoch. He is now best known for his strictures as a literary and cultural critic, and educationist. After a long period of neglect, his views have come in for a re-evaluation. Arnold's poetry remains less well known, yet his poems and his understanding of poetry, which defied the conventions of his time, were central to his achievement.
The author traces Arnold's intellectual and poetic development, showing how his poetry gathers its meanings from a lifetime's study of European literature and philosophy. Connolly's unique exegesis of 'Thyrsis' draws upon a wide-ranging analysis of the pastoral and its associated myths in both classical and native cultures. This study shows lucidly and in detail how Arnold encouraged the intense reflection of the mind on the subject placed before it, believing in " … the all importance of the choice of the subject, the necessity of accurate observation; and subordinate character of expression."

Patrick Carill Connolly gained his English degree at Reading University and taught English literature abroad for a number of years before returning to Britain. He is now a civil servant living in London.

2004 • 180 pages • ISBN 978-1-871551-61-7

The Author, the Book and the Reader *by Robert Giddings*
This collection of essays analyses the effects of changing technology and the attendant commercial pressures on literary styles and subject matter. Authors covered include Charles Dickens, Tobias Smollett, Mark Twain, Dr Johnson and John le Carré.

1991 • 220 pages • illustrated • ISBN 978-1-871551-01-3

Norman Cameron *by Warren Hope*
Cameron's poetry was admired by Auden; celebrated by Dylan Thomas; valued by Robert Graves. He was described by Martin Seymour-Smith as "one of ... the most rewarding and pure poets of his generation ..." and is at last given a full-length biography. This eminently sociable man, who had periods of darkness and despair, wrote little poetry by comparison with others of his time, but always of a consistently high quality – imaginative and profound.
Warren Hope is a poet, a critic and university lecturer. He lives and works in Philadelphia, where he raised his family.

2000 • 226 pages • ISBN 978-1-871551-05-1

Aleister Crowley and the Cult of Pan *by Paul Newman*
Few more nightmarish figures stalk English literature than Aleister Crowley (1875-1947), poet, magician, mountaineer and agent provocateur. In this groundbreaking study, Paul Newman dives into the occult mire of Crowley's works and fishes out gems and grotesqueries that are by turns ethereal, sublime, pornographic and horrifying. Like Oscar Wilde before him, Crowley stood in "symbolic relationship to his age" and to contemporaries like Rupert Brooke, G.K. Chesterton and the Portuguese modernist, Fernando Pessoa. An influential exponent of the cult of the Great God Pan, his essentially 'pagan' outlook was shared by major European writers as well as English novelists like E.M. Forster, D.H. Lawrence and Arthur Machen.
Paul Newman lives in Cornwall. Editor of the literary magazine *Abraxas*, he has written over ten books.

2004 • 222 pages • ISBN 978-1-871551-66-2

John Dryden *by Anthony Fowles*

Of all the poets of the Augustan age, John Dryden was the most worldly. Anthony Fowles traces Dryden's evolution from 'wordsmith' to major poet. This critical study shows a poet of vigour and technical panache whose art was forged in the heat and battle of a turbulent polemical and pamphleteering age. Although Dryden's status as a literary critic has long been established, Fowles draws attention to his neglected achievements as a translator of poetry. He deals also with the less well-known aspects of Dryden's work – his plays and occasional pieces.

Born in London and educated at the Universities of Oxford and Southern California, Anthony Fowles began his career in film-making before becoming an author of film and television scripts and more than twenty books. Readers will welcome the many contemporary references to novels and film with which Fowles illuminates the life and work of this decisively influential English poetic voice.

2003 • 292 pages • ISBN 978-1-871551-58-7

The Good That We Do *by John Lucas*

John Lucas' book blends fiction, biography and social history in order to tell the story of his grandfather, Horace Kelly. Headteacher of a succession of elementary schools in impoverished areas of London, 'Hod' Kelly was also a keen cricketer, a devotee of the music hall, and included among his friends the great trade union leader Ernest Bevin. In telling the story of his life, Lucas has provided a fascinating range of insights into the lives of ordinary Londoners from the First World War until the outbreak of the Second World War. Threaded throughout is an account of such people's hunger for education, and of the different ways government, church and educational officialdom ministered to that hunger. *The Good That We Do* is both a study of one man and of a period when England changed, drastically and forever.

John Lucas is Professor Emeritus of the Universities of Loughborough and Nottingham Trent. He is the author of numerous works of a critical and scholarly nature and has published eight collections of poetry.

2001 • 214 pages • ISBN 978-1-871551-54-9

D.H. Lawrence: The Nomadic Years, 1919-1930 *by Philip Callow*

This book provides a fresh insight into Lawrence's art as well as his life. Candid about the relationship between Lawrence and his wife, it shows nevertheless the strength of the bond between them. If no other book persuaded the reader of Lawrence's greatness, this does.

Philip Callow was born in Birmingham and studied engineering and teaching before he turned to writing. He has published 14 novels, several collections of short stories and poems, a volume of autobiography, and biographies on the lives of Chekhov, Cezanne, Robert Louis Stevenson, Walt Whitman and Van Gogh all of which have received critical acclaim. His biography of D.H. Lawrence's early years, *Son and Lover*, was widely praised.

2006 • 226 pages • ISBN 978-1-871551-82-2

Liar! Liar!: Jack Kerouac – Novelist *by R.J. Ellis*
The fullest study of Jack Kerouac's fiction to date. It is the first book to devote an individual chapter to every one of his novels. *On the Road*, *Visions of Cody* and *The Subterraneans* are reread in-depth, in a new and exciting way. *Visions of Gerard* and *Doctor Sax* are also strikingly reinterpreted, as are other daringly innovative writings, like 'The Railroad Earth' and his "try at a spontaneous *Finnegans Wake*" – *Old Angel Midnight*. Neglected writings, such as *Tristessa* and *Big Sur*, are also analysed, alongside better-known novels such as *Dharma Bums* and *Desolation Angels*.
R.J. Ellis is Senior Lecturer in English at Nottingham Trent University.

1999 • 294 pages • ISBN 978-1-871551-53-2

In Pursuit of Lewis Carroll *by Raphael Shaberman*
Sherlock Holmes and the author uncover new evidence in their investigations into the mysterious life and writing of Lewis Carroll. They examine published works by Carroll that have been overlooked by previous commentators. A newly-discovered poem, almost certainly by Carroll, is published here.
Amongst many aspects of Carroll's highly complex personality, this book explores his relationship with his parents, numerous child friends, and the formidable Mrs Liddell, mother of the immortal Alice. Raphael Shaberman was a founder member of the Lewis Carroll Society and a teacher of autistic children.

1994 • 118 pages • illustrated • ISBN 978-1-871551-13-6

Poetry in Exile: A study of the poetry of W.H. Auden, Joseph Brodsky & George Szirtes *by Michael Murphy*
"Michael Murphy discriminates the forms of exile and expatriation with the shrewdness of the cultural historian, the acuity of the literary critic, and the subtlety of a poet alert to the ways language and poetic form embody the precise contours of experience. His accounts of Auden, Brodsky and Szirtes not only cast much new light on the work of these complex and rewarding poets, but are themselves a pleasure to read." *Stan Smith, Research Professor in Literary Studies, Nottingham Trent University.*
Michael Murphy is a poet and critic. He teaches English literature at Liverpool Hope University College.

2004 • 266 pages • ISBN 978-1-871551-76-1

Wordsworth and Coleridge: Views from the Meticulous to the Sublime
by Andrew Keanie
For a long time the received view of the collaborative relationship between Wordsworth and Coleridge has been that Wordsworth was the efficient producer of more finished poetic statements (most notably his long, autobiographical poem *The Prelude*) and Coleridge, however extraordinary he was as a thinker and a talker, left behind more intolerably diffuse and fragmented works. *Wordsworth and Coleridge: Views from the Meticulous to the Sublime* examines the issue from a number of different critical vantage points, reassessing the poets' inextricable achievements, and rediscovering their legacy.
Andrew Keanie is a lecturer at the University of Ulster. He is the author of articles on William Wordsworth, Samuel Taylor Coleridge and Hartley Coleridge. He has written three books for the Greenwich Exchange *Student Guide Literary Series* on Wordsworth, Coleridge and Byron.
2007 • 206 pages • hardback • ISBN 978-1-871551-87-7

STUDENT GUIDE LITERARY SERIES

The Greenwich Exchange Student Guide Literary Series is a collection of critical essays of major or contemporary serious writers in English and selected European languages. The series is for the student, the teacher and 'common readers' and is an ideal resource for libraries. The *Times Educational Supplement* praised these books, saying, "The style of [this series] has a pressure of meaning behind it. Readers should learn from that … If art is about selection, perception and taste, then this is it."

(ISBN prefix 978-1-871551 applies unless marked* when 978-1-906075 applies).

All books are paperback.

The series includes:
Antonin Artaud by Lee Jamieson (98-3)
W.H. Auden by Stephen Wade (36-5)
Honoré de Balzac by Wendy Mercer (48-8)
William Blake by Peter Davies (27-3)
The Brontës by Peter Davies (24-2)
Robert Browning by John Lucas (59-4)
Lord Byron by Andrew Keanie (83-9)
Samuel Taylor Coleridge by Andrew Keanie (64-8)
Joseph Conrad by Martin Seymour-Smith (18-1)

William Cowper by Michael Thorn (25-9)
Charles Dickens by Robert Giddings (26-9)
Emily Dickinson by Marnie Pomeroy (68-6)
John Donne by Sean Haldane (23-5)
Ford Madox Ford by Anthony Fowles (63-1)
The Stagecraft of Brian Friel by David Grant (74-7)
Robert Frost by Warren Hope (70-9)
Patrick Hamilton by John Harding (99-0)
Thomas Hardy by Sean Haldane (33-4)
Seamus Heaney by Warren Hope (37-2)
Joseph Heller by Anthony Fowles (84-6)
Gerard Manley Hopkins by Sean Sheehan (77-3)
James Joyce by Michael Murphy (73-0)
Philip Larkin by Warren Hope (35-8)
Laughter in the Dark – The Plays of Joe Orton by Arthur Burke (56-3)
George Orwell byWarren Hope (42-6)
Sylvia Plath by Marnie Pomeroy (88-4)
Poets of the First World War by John Greening (79-2)
Philip Roth by Paul McDonald (72-3)
Shakespeare's *King Lear* by Peter Davies (95-2)
Shakespeare's *Macbeth* by Matt Simpson (69-3)
Shakespeare's *The Merchant of Venice* by Alan Ablewhite (96-9)
Shakespeare's *A Midsummer Night's Dream* by Matt Simpson (90-7)
Shakespeare's *Much Ado About Nothing* by Matt Simpson (01-9)*
Shakespeare's Non-Dramatic Poetry by Martin Seymour-Smith (22-6)
Shakespeare's *Othello* by Matt Simpson (71-6)
Shakespeare's Second Tetralogy: *Richard II – Henry V* by John Lucas (97-6)
Shakespeare's Sonnets by Martin Seymour-Smith (38-9)
Shakespeare's *The Tempest* by Matt Simpson (75-4)
Shakespeare's *Twelfth Night* by Matt Simpson (86-0)
Shakespeare's *The Winter's Tale* by John Lucas (80-3)
Tobias Smollett by Robert Giddings (21-1)
Alfred, Lord Tennyson by Michael Thorn (20-4)
Dylan Thomas by Peter Davies (78-5)
William Wordsworth by Andrew Keanie (57-0)
W.B. Yeats by John Greening (34-1)